What Will I Do With
All Those Root Vegetables?

D1612800

Elaine Borish, an American living in London, was born in New York City. She holds degrees from Rutgers, Boston University, and Northeastern University and has taught at universities in New England. In old England, she has lectured in English and American literature at Morley College in London. Her numerous articles have appeared in leading newspapers and magazines.

Also by Elaine Borish

A Legacy of Names
Literary Lodgings
Novel Cuisine
This Book Is Unpublishable!
What Will I Do With All Those Courgettes?
What Will I Do With All Those Zucchini?

Elaine Borish

What Will I Do With All Those Root Vegetables?

Fidelio Press

Telluride • London

For all dedicated lovers and growers of root vegetables—
especially one man with a hoe, my husband

Published by
Fidelio Press, Inc.
129 Aldasoro Road
Telluride CO 81435

Printed in United States of America

Cover design by Kate Chitham

PREFACE

Vegetables are a great feature in today's culinary world, and most varieties are available to us most of the time. But the home grower has the advantage of obtaining the youngest and freshest and knows that the pleasure of eating these real delicacies is in the flavor.

After publication of my first volume, "What Will I Do With All Those Courgettes?" friends and gardening acquaintances began to entreat: But what should I do with my parsnips? What about my Jerusalem artichokes? I grew too many carrots. I had to give away half my radishes. I had a bumper crop of beets. . . what should I do? My family is tired of all those. . . . Oh no, not turnips again! And so on.

The litany left me with little choice but to prepare another book for easy-to-grow vegetables using easy-to-prepare recipes. In general, root vegetables are easiest to grow and, let's face it, easy-to-grow vegetables call for easy-to-prepare recipes.

I have tried to offer recipes that are unusual, or less ordinary, as well as easy. Although potatoes might form a cookery book on their own, the dishes selected are not the conventional day-to-day fare but will go a long way toward using up your crop while producing festive food for your table.

My favorite word in specifying recipe quantities or instructions remains "about" because preparation should be easy and fun. I still believe that undue concern for exactness should not outweigh your own logical application.

Contents

Beetroot or Beets

BEETROOT or BEETS

Beetroot is referred to as beets by Americans, and I use the terms interchangeably. Beets can be used for soup or salad, or they can be boiled or baked for use as a hot vegetable. Or pickled. Even the young leaves can be cooked, as for spinach or chard, and are hardly distinguishable from chard. Beet greens are extremely nutritious, being high in vitamins A and C as well as iron and calcium. That the leaves are not otherwise easily available, is one great advantage of growing your own.

Beets grow from spring through autumn but are available year round. They store well and are all right for freezing.

When preparing whole beets for cooking, scrub them well but leave on at least one inch of stems and root ends, being careful not to break the skin as they bleed easily. Cook in boiling water to cover, with lid on, until tender (test with skewer or fork). Drain and slip off the skins. If you are lucky enough to have your own beet greens, boil them for a few minutes, then drain well, and add some butter or olive oil before serving.

Beets might be used more frequently if they weren't so messy to handle, staining hands and the materials they touch. It is nevertheless worth handling this delicious root, which is also a good natural source of potassium.

For a practical way of preparing beets for use, see Baked Beets in Foil (page 17). Simply wash the beets well and wrap each one in aluminum foil. Place on a baking sheet and bake in hot oven for ¾ to 1½ hours, depending on size. They are done when easily pierced with a skewer. They can be frozen or kept refrigerated for a few days until ready to use.

RECIPES for BEETROOT OR BEETS

Russian Borscht

There are literally dozens of different ways to make Russian borscht, or beet soup. The only unvarying ingredient is beetroot, from which is derived the name and color. Here is an easy recipe for a hot and hearty and thick borscht.

2½ lbs (1.1 kg) lean beef, cut into small cubes
20 fl oz (600 ml or 2 ½ cups) water
1 medium onion
1 teaspoon salt
8-10 peppercorns
1 bay leaf
1 lb (500g) fresh beets, peeled and finely shredded
½ small head cabbage, shredded
1 large tin tomatoes
1-2 medium onions, thinly sliced
salt and pepper to taste
1 tablespoon lemon juice
sour cream (optional)

1. Bring the beef, water, onion, salt, peppercorns, and bay leaf to a boil, then simmer covered for 1½ hours. Remove and discard the onion, peppercorns, and bay leaf.
2. To the beef and broth, add the beets, cabbage, tomatoes, and onions. Bring to a boil and simmer covered 1-1½ hours or until all ingredients are tender.
3. Add salt and pepper. Add lemon juice and adjust the seasonings.
4. If you want to, add a spoonful of sour cream to each bowl before serving. Or pass the sour cream around for guests to help themselves.

Serves 8

Cold Borscht

The distinctive sweet and sour flavor of this cool beetroot soup makes it a popular favorite, and the sour cream adds an authentic Russian touch.

2 lbs (1 kg) beetroots
70 fl oz (3½ pints or 2 litres) water
salt and pepper
juice of 1 lemon
1-2 tablespoons sugar, according to taste
10 oz (300 ml) sour cream
chives, to garnish
6 peeled boiled potatoes (optional)

1. Peel and grate the raw beetroots using a coarse grater or food processor. Put them in a saucepan with water and salt and pepper. Simmer for 1½ hours.
2. Allow to cool. Then add lemon and sugar to taste. Cover and chill in refrigerator.
3. When ready to serve, float a tablespoon of thick sour cream in each bowl and garnish with a sprinkling of chopped chives. Or pass the sour cream at the table for guests to help themselves.
5. Another option is to serve with a hot boiled potato on a plate, alongside the soup.

Serves 8

Another Borscht

What a wonderfully vibrant and vivid vegetarian soup!

4 small beets (about 12 oz or 300 g)
1 onion, diced
2 cloves garlic, chopped
1 small potato, peeled and diced
1 oz (25 g) butter
dash of olive oil
25 fl oz (750 ml) vegetable stock
pinch of cumin
2 tablespoons cider vinegar
salt and freshly ground pepper to taste
crème fraîche and chopped parsley for garnish

1. Prepare the beetroot. Remove the top, peel off the skin, and cut into small pieces.
2. Peel and dice the onion and potato.
3. Melt the butter in a large saucepan with a dash of olive oil. Add the diced onion and sauté for 5 minutes until soft. Stir in the prepared beetroot, potato, and garlic. Cook for another five minutes.
4. Season with cumin and black pepper. Pour in the vegetable stock. Bring to a boil, then reduce heat and simmer covered for 1 hour.
5. When vegetables are soft, process mixture to the consistency you want. Mix in the cider vinegar and adjust the seasonings.
6. Serve hot, garnished with a dollop of crème fraîche and parsley.

Serves 4

Vegetarian Beet Soup

This delicious and heart-healthy soup contains no fat. You have the option of adding a dollop of sour cream to serve it like traditional borscht.

6 medium beets, peeled and coarsely shredded
1 large carrot, coarsely shredded
1 medium onion, finely chopped
½ small head cabbage, finely shredded
32 fl oz (1 litre or 4 cups) water
¼ teaspoon salt
pepper to taste
½ teaspoon paprika
1 tablespoon lemon juice

1. Combine all ingredients *except* lemon juice in a large saucepan.
2. Bring to a boil over medium heat. Reduce heat, cover, and simmer 30 minutes.
3. Stir in lemon juice and serve. (Garnish with a dollop of sour cream if desired.)

Serves 6

Beets and Roots Soup

My friend Lou created this soup from vegetables that he wanted to use up. You can be as creative as Lou and use celery and green or red pepper—or whatever.

4 tablespoons vegetable oil
3 medium beets, diced
2 medium onions, diced
4 carrots, diced
2 parsnips, diced
1 teaspoon plus 1 teaspoon dried thyme
½ plus ½ teaspoon dried rosemary
½ plus ½ teaspoon ground coriander
2 bay leaves, crumbled
1 apple, peeled and diced
1-2 cloves garlic, finely diced
42 fl oz (1.2 litres) chicken broth
16 fl oz (500 ml or 2 cups) water
1 tin garbanzo beans, drained
sour cream and parsley to garnish

1. Measure oil into a large soup pot and sauté beets, onions, carrots, and parsnips with 1 teaspoon thyme, ½ teaspoon rosemary, ½ teaspoon coriander and bay leaves. As vegetables begin to soften, add apple. Cook until all vegetables are soft.
2. Add garlic, broth, and water. Blend in 1 teaspoon thyme, ½ teaspoon rosemary, and ½ teaspoon coriander.
3. Taste for flavoring. For more sweetness, add a second diced apple. Add more herbs if necessary. Cook until blended.
4. Purée mixture coarsely in a food processor and return to pot. Add drained garbanzo beans and reheat when ready to serve.
5. Serve with a dollop of sour cream and a parsley sprig.

Serves 10

Beet and Spring Onion Appetizer

This easy-to-prepare and attractive-looking appetizer may be served on chilled plates.

3-4 medium beets, cooked
2-3 spring onions, chopped
½ teaspoon mustard
4 oz (100 g or ½ cup) sour cream or crème fraîche
½ teaspoon lemon juice
freshly ground black pepper, to taste

1. Cut the beets into thin strips like matches, or chop coarsely. Add the spring onions.
2. Mix the remaining ingredients together and add to the beets. Blend. Chill. Serve with toast.

Serves 4

Marinated Beetroot Salad

Another salad that is easy to prepare and good to eat.

1 lb (450 g) fresh beetroot, boiled, peeled, thinly sliced
1 small red onion, thinly sliced
2 tablespoons soy sauce
2 tablespoons red wine vinegar
1 teaspoon grated fresh ginger
1 teaspoon grated orange rind
¼ teaspoon pepper

1. Layer the beets and onion in a serving bowl.
2. Combine soy sauce, wine vinegar, ginger, orange rind and pepper in a bowl and whisk until well mixed. Pour mixture over the prepared layers.
3. Chill in refrigerator, covered, for at least 1 hour. Stir gently before serving.

Serves 4

Pickled Beetroot

This old recipe makes a great side dish or a spicy addition to a tossed salad and will keep for weeks in the refrigerator.

2 lbs (1 kg) beetroot
12 fl oz (350 ml or 1½ cups) cider vinegar
1½ tablespoons dry mustard
½ teaspoon salt
5 oz (150 g) sugar
2 medium onions, sliced (optional)
2 teaspoons celery seed

1. Wash the beetroot carefully without damaging the skins. Cook in water to cover until tender. Set aside 8 oz (225 ml or 1 cup) of the cooking water. Slip skins off beets and slice.
2. Combine the vinegar and reserved cooking water and bring to a boil. Mix the mustard, salt and sugar. Add to vinegar and allow to boil again.
3. Arrange the beets and onions in layers packed into jars. Add the celery seed and cover with the hot vinegar mixture. Seal, cool and store in refrigerator. Allow to stand for a few days before using.

Makes about 3 pints

Russian Beet Salad

Be sure that this delicious salad, which takes about an hour to prepare, is well chilled before serving.

8 small (2 ½-inch diameter) beets
4 fl oz (100 ml or ½ cup) cider vinegar
1 clove garlic, crushed
2 teaspoons honey
1 small-medium red onion, finely chopped
2 spring onions, finely chopped
1 small cucumber, seeded and finely chopped
2 hardboiled eggs, chopped
2 tablespoons fresh dill, minced (or 1 teaspoon dried dill)
about 16 oz (475 ml or 2 cups) sour cream
salt and pepper

1. Boil the beets, whole, for about 20-25 minutes until tender. Rub off the skins and cut into ½ inch (1.2 cm) cubes.
2. While the beets are still warm, marinate them in the vinegar, garlic and honey. Allow to stand for 30 minutes.
3. Mix in all remaining ingredients and toss to thoroughly combine. Chill until cold before serving.

Serves 4-5

Beetroot and Fennel Salad

The contrasting textures of crunchy fennel and smooth beets combine with flavors that produce an impressive salad.

4 medium beets
1 bulb fennel
2 tablespoons olive oil
1 tablespoon fresh lemon juice
1 tablespoon minced fresh basil leaves or 1 teaspoon minced
 fresh tarragon leaves or ½ teaspoon dried tarragon
salt and pepper to taste

1. Wash the beets, wrap each in foil and place on a baking sheet or in a roasting pan. Bake for 45-90 minutes, or until tender when pierced with a skewer.
2. Trim the fennel and chop into ½-1 inch (1.5-2.5 cm) pieces.
3. Peel the beets and chop into pieces about the same size as the fennel.
4. Toss beets and fennel together with the remaining ingredients and serve. If you keep the salad for a while before serving, the fennel will turn red. Garnish with chopped herbs if you want to.

Serves 4-6

Beet Salad Mold

This aspic can definitely be prepared a day ahead of your planned dinner.

1 lb (450 g) cooked julienne beets
1 tablespoon unflavored gelatin
2 tablespoons sugar
4 fl oz (100 ml) water
juice of half a lemon
½ teaspoon vinegar
1½ teaspoons horseradish
1 stalk celery, finely chopped

1. Prepare and cook beets. Drain beets and cut them into julienne strips. Set aside 8 oz (225 ml or 1 cup) of the cooked beet water.
2. Mix gelatin, sugar, and water in a saucepan. Heat, stirring until gelatin is dissolved. Remove from heat.
3. Mix lemon juice, vinegar, and horseradish into the reserved cooking liquid and add to the gelatin mixture.
4. Refrigerate until mixture is slightly thickened, then add beets and celery. Stir well and pour into a mold. Refrigerate.
5. Unmold salad and serve.

Beetroot Chutney

Chutneys are served as condiments in Indian meals, but this chutney can enliven any main dish such as grilled meats or roast chicken.

2 apples, cored and sliced
1 onion, peeled and sliced
4 fl oz (120 ml) raspberry or red wine vinegar
2 teaspoons freshly grated root ginger
1 teaspoon ground allspice
2 whole cloves
1 lb (450 g) cooked beetroot
2 oz (50 g) brown sugar
2 oz (50 g) raisins

1. Place sliced apples and onions into a large pot. Add vinegar, root ginger, allspice, and cloves. Bring to a boil. Then reduce heat and simmer for 20 minutes, stirring occasionally.
2. Cook beetroots by adding them to a pan of boiling salted water, then simmering for 20-30 minutes. Drain and cool. Peel them and chop them finely. Add to the apple-onion mixture.
3. Bring to a boil, then simmer for 15 minutes.
4. Allow to cool. Cover and refrigerate until ready to use.

Serves 10

Beet Preserves

What an interesting and conversation-making way to use a large crop of beets! It's also delicious.

3 lbs (1.4 kg) beets
sugar, as needed
1-2 lemons, thinly sliced
8 oz (225 g or 1 cup) chopped walnuts
½ teaspoon ground ginger

1. Cut beets into matchstick strips and soak overnight in cold water.
2. Drain beets, reserving water. Place them in a heavy saucepan and add just enough water to cover beets. Bring to a boil. Add sugar in equal proportion to beets.
3. Bring to a slow boil, stirring until mixture jells. Add sliced lemons and chopped walnuts and cook for another 5 minutes.
4. Remove from heat. Add ginger. Spoon into hot, sterile jars.

Serves 12

Baked Beets in Foil

This is the best way to cook beets. It reduces messiness and staining and offers the option of storing them for use days later. When you are ready, just remove the foil and peel them. Re-cook or use cold.

1½-2 lbs (700 g-1 kg) beets (4 large or 8 medium)
butter or vinaigrette or lemon juice (optional)

1. Wash beets well and wrap them individually in foil.
2. Place on a baking sheet or in a roasting pan and bake in oven preheated to 400°F (200°C) for 45 minutes to 1½ hours, depending on size, until they can be easily pierced with a skewer. Remove each one as done.
3. To serve right away, peel, then slice or cut them into chunks. Melt about 2 tablespoons butter in a large frying pan and cook the beets for about 5 minutes, stirring until hot. Or drizzle vinaigrette or fresh lemon juice over them. Or cool and refrigerate them for up to a few days, until ready to use according to any recipe.

Serves 4-6

Sautéed Beetroot

A little imagination makes this root vegetable a welcome accompaniment to a winter meal.

1 large beetroot, cooked
1½ oz (40 g) butter
2 tablespoons finely chopped onion
1 clove garlic, crushed
salt and pepper to taste
sugar to taste
1 tablespoon of mild vinegar

1. Cut the cooked beetroot into shreds.
2. Melt butter in a heavy pan and add onion and garlic, cooking until soft. Add shredded beetroot. Season with salt and pepper. Add sugar (if you want to) and vinegar.
3. Warm through and serve.

Serves 3-4

Beetroot-Apple Purée

Add zest to the dinner plate with this bright and tempting offering that goes well with almost any entrée.

about 2 lbs (1 kg) medium beets
8 tablespoons (4 oz or 110 g) butter
1 medium-large onion, finely chopped
4 tart apples
1 tablespoon sugar
½ teaspoon salt
2 fl oz (50 ml or ¼ cup) raspberry vinegar
chopped fresh dill (optional)

1. Scrub beets well and place them in a saucepan of salted water. Bring to a boil, then reduce heat and simmer until beets are tender (about 40 minutes). Add more water if necessary to keep beets covered. When done, drain the beets, cool, and rub off the skins.
2. Melt the butter in a saucepan. Add onions, cover and cook until tender—about 10 minutes.
3. Add the apples, which have been peeled, cored, and chopped. Add sugar, salt, and raspberry vinegar. Add dill if desired. Simmer, uncovered, for about 15 minutes, until apples are tender.
4. Chop beets and place in a food processor together with the apple-onion mixture. Process until smooth.
5. To serve hot, return to the saucepan and stir continuously while reheating. Correct seasonings and serve. To serve cold, transfer to a bowl, cover, and refrigerate until well chilled.

Serves 8

Beetroot with Orange Marmalade

*The combination of cooked beetroot with orange marmalade
makes a surprisingly flavorful blend that goes especially well
with game, duck, or goose. Delicious—and easy!*

**1 lb (450 g) cooked beetroot
1 oz (25 g) butter
1 heaping tablespoon marmalade
juice of half an orange**

1. Skin the beetroot and cut into cubes.
2. In a saucepan, heat the butter, marmalade and orange juice
   until the butter melts. Then add the beetroot.
3. Simmer gently for 10 minutes, stirring occasionally, until the
   liquid has evaporated.
4. Spoon it into a hot serving dish, garnish with a slice of orange,
   and serve.

Serves 4

Beets With Orange

Another way to use orange with beets—a good combination.

4 oz (110 g or ½ cup) sugar
1 tablespoon cornstarch
½ teaspoon salt
4 fl oz (100 ml or ½ cup) cider vinegar
2 tablespoons water
grated rind and juice of 1 orange
6 medium beets, cooked and sliced
3 tablespoons butter

1. In a saucepan mix together the sugar, cornstarch, salt, vinegar and water. (Use less sugar if you want to.) Bring to a boil. Stir until clear.
2. Add the orange rind and juice and stir in the beets. Heat gently and stir in the butter before serving.

Serves 6

Baked Beets in Cream and Lemon

The vivid color of beetroot enhances the dinner plate in a spectacular way.

2 lbs (1 kg) beetroot, cooked and thinly sliced
grated rind of 1 lemon
5 fl oz (150 ml) single or light cream
salt and pepper
2 tablespoons breadcrumbs

1. Arrange the beetroot slices, overlapping each other, in a shallow, buttered ovenproof dish.
2. Sprinkle the lemon rind over it. Pour the cream over the top and season with salt and freshly ground black pepper.
3. Bake in a moderate oven at 350°F (180°C) for 20 minutes.
4. Remove from oven, sprinkle breadcrumbs over it, and put under a hot grill to toast the crumbs.

Serves 6

Gingered Beetroot

Another spicy way to lend interest to a serving of beets.

5-6 medium beets, cooked and cubed
3 oz (75 g or 1/3 cup) sugar
¾ teaspoon ground ginger
2 teaspoons cornstarch
2 fl oz (50 ml or ¼ cup) cider vinegar
2 tablespoons butter
1 tablespoon chopped parsley

1. Prepare and cook the beets
2. Combine sugar, ginger and cornstarch in a saucepan. Slowly add the vinegar, stirring until smooth. Cook over medium heat, stirring until thickened.
3. Add the beets and butter. Simmer for 10 minutes, stirring occasionally.
4. Serve hot, sprinkled with chopped parsley.

Serves 4-6

Sweet and Sour Beets

This accompaniment can also be served cold.

6-8 medium beets (about 1½ lbs or 700 g), cooked and sliced
6 fl oz (175 ml or ¾ cup) reserved cooking liquid plus 2
  tablespoons
6 oz (175 g or ¾ cup) raisins
1 tablespoon corn starch
2-3 tablespoons sugar
3 tablespoons butter
juice of one lemon
chopped spring onion (for garnish)

1. Cook beets and slice them, reserving the liquid in which they are cooked.
2. Combine 6 oz (175 ml) beet liquid with raisins in a saucepan. Bring to a boil, reduce heat, and simmer covered for about 5 minutes.
3. Blend corn starch with 2 tablespoons beet liquid and stir into raisin mixture. Add sugar and butter. Omit butter if serving cold. Cook over low heat, stirring constantly until butter is melted and sugar is dissolved.
4. Add lemon juice and beets and cook until heated through.
5. Garnish with chopped spring onions and serve.

Serves 6-8

Beet Roesti

With its blend of flavors, and with the caramelization of the beet sugar, this dish of roesti (beet cakes) makes an absolutely delicious accompaniment.

1-1 ½ lbs (450-700 g) beets, grated
1 teaspoon fresh rosemary, chopped
salt, to taste
5 tablespoons (about ¼ cup) flour
2 tablespoons butter

1. Trim and peel the beets. Grate them in a food processor.
2. In a bowl, mix together beets, rosemary and salt. Add about half the flour and mix well. Add remainder of the flour and mix again.
3. Heat butter in a preheated non-stick frying pan until it begins to brown. Spoon beet mixture into the pan and shape it into a circle, pressing down with a spatula.
4. Cook on medium to high heat until bottom of beet cake is crisp, about 6-8 minutes. Then turn it over: Slide the cake onto a plate, put another plate over it, turn the two plates over, and slide the cake back into the pan with the uncooked side down. Continue to cook until bottom is browned.
5. Cut into wedges and serve.

Serves 4

Stuffed Beetroot

*Use the scooped-out part of the beets for some other recipe,
such as borscht or beet and spring onion appetizer.*

6 medium beets, cooked, peeled, and chilled
4 fl oz (100 ml or ½ cup) cider vinegar
**6 fl oz (150 ml or ¾ cup) water in which the beets were
    cooked (add more water if necessary)**
1 teaspoon salt
1 teaspoon sugar
4 hard-boiled eggs, coarsely chopped
2 teaspoons chives, finely chopped
3 teaspoons chopped parsley
4 oz (100 g or ½ cup) mayonnaise
freshly ground black pepper

1. Using a melon cutter or sharp spoon, hollow the beets, leaving
   a fairly thin rim.
2. Mix together the vinegar and beet juice water. Add salt and
   sugar and cover the beet shells with the mixture.
3. Chill in refrigerator for at least one hour.
4. Combine remaining ingredients.
5. Stuff the beets with the mixture just before serving and serve
   on a bed of endive or lettuce.

Serves 6

Carrots

CARROTS

It was during the reign of Elizabeth I that the Dutch first brought this vegetable to England. They were still a novelty in the English court of the 1700s and prized for their feathery green foliage, reputedly worn sometimes on ladies' hats. But recipes exist dating from Roman times when they were appreciated for their sweetness and color.

The popular and versatile carrot is a year-round staple that stores well. However, young carrots of spring and early summer are the most sweet, tender, and flavorful. To prepare carrots, top and tail and scrub in cold water. Scrape young carrots, peel old ones.

The natural sweetness of carrots makes them delicious eaten raw and crunchy or lightly cooked. Among a wide variety of uses are soups, snacks, salads, stews and casseroles. Carrots may be stir-fried or simply boiled or steamed as a vegetable (for 10 to 15 minutes depending on size and age). Carrot soups are simple to make and yield a lovely rich color. The soup thickens when puréed but should be liquidized thoroughly for a smooth consistency. Less common uses include pickled carrots, chutney, and cake.

Carrots are among the most nourishing and inexpensive vegetables. They are an excellent source of Vitamin A as well as B3, C, and E. Raw carrots provide significant quantities of potassium, calcium, iron, and zinc.

RECIPES for CARROTS

MISCELLANEOUS

Carrot Soup

This velvety thick carrot soup makes a good spontaneous choice because not only is it simple to make but the ingredients are probably available. For a deeper color and an effective change of flavor, add a little concentrated tomato purée.

1 medium onion, chopped
2-3 cloves garlic, minced
2 tablespoons vegetable oil
1 teaspoon thyme
8 medium carrots, thinly sliced
2 medium potatoes, peeled and diced
1 bay leaf
1 teaspoon salt
freshly ground pepper to taste
35 fl oz or 1 litre chicken stock

1. In a large saucepan, sauté the onion and garlic in oil over low heat until soft.
2. Stir in thyme. Mix in carrots, potatoes, bay leaf, salt, and pepper. Cover and cook, stirring occasionally, for another 10 minutes.
3. Add the stock. Bring to a boil, then cover and simmer until vegetables are tender, about 15-20 minutes.
4. Purée soup in a blender or food processor.
5. Return to saucepan and heat thoroughly. Serve hot, garnished with chopped parsley.

Serves 8-10

Carrot and Orange Soup

As home-grown carrots become more plentiful, it is well worth trying this orange-flavored carrot soup, which may become a regular in your dinner party repertoire.

4 tablespoons butter
2 small-medium onions, finely chopped
2 lbs (1 kg) carrots), chopped
32 fl oz (1 litre or 4 cups) chicken stock
8 fl oz (200 ml or 1 cup) orange juice
salt and freshly ground black pepper to taste
grated fresh orange rind to taste

1. In a large pot, melt the butter and add the onions. Cover and cook over low heat until tender and golden, about 20 minutes.
2. Add carrots and stock. Bring to a boil, then reduce heat. Simmer covered about 30 minutes or until carrots are tender.
3. Strain the soup and reserve the liquid. Purée the solids in a food processor with 1 cup of the cooking stock until smooth.
4. Return purée to the pot. Add orange juice and 2 to 3 cups of additional cooking stock, as necessary, until soup is of the desired consistency.
5. Season to taste with salt and pepper. Add orange rind.
6. Heat through when ready to serve.

Serves 6 to 8

Carrot and Coriander Soup

*This uncomplicated, low-calorie soup uses coriander, which
goes well with carrots.*

4 large carrots, peeled and chopped
2 oz (50 g) butter
1 large onion, peeled and finely chopped
1 potato, peeled and chopped
2 tablespoons (or less) coriander seeds
35 fl oz (1 litre) chicken stock
salt and freshly ground black pepper to taste
finely chopped parsley

1. Peel and chop the carrots.
2. Melt the butter in a saucepan on a low heat. Add the chopped
   onion and cook until soft. Stir in the carrots, potato and
   coriander. (Tie coriander seeds in a gauze sac for easy
   removal.) Cook for about 5 minutes, stirring occasionally.
3. Pour in the stock and season with salt and pepper. Bring to a
   boil, cover, and simmer gently for 30-40 minutes, or until
   vegetables are tender.
4. Cool slightly. Remove coriander seeds. Purée soup in a food
   processor or blender. You may sieve the soup if you want to
   remove any bits of coriander that are not broken down by the
   blender.
5. Reheat when ready to serve, stirring some finely chopped
   parsley into the soup just before serving.

Serves 6

Chilled Carrot Soup

Chilled soups are especially elegant on a summer evening. This one may also be served hot, but the subtle creaminess is enhanced when the soup is chilled.

1 medium onion, thinly sliced
1-2 cloves garlic, crushed
1 oz (25 g) butter
4 large carrots (about 1½ lbs or 650 g), chopped
35 fl oz (1 litre or 4 cups) chicken stock
8 fl oz (200 ml or 1 cup) heavy or double cream
salt and black pepper
finely chopped parsley for garnish

1. Sauté the onion and garlic in butter over low heat in a covered saucepan until soft and lightly coloured.
2. Add the carrots and continue cooking, covered, until vegetables are soft, about 6-8 minutes.
3. Add half the stock and simmer for about 30 minutes.
4. Allow soup to cool slightly, then transfer to a food processor or blender and purée until smooth. Return to pan.
5. Add remaining stock. Stir cream into the soup and season to taste with salt and freshly ground black pepper. Chill.
6. Serve in individual bowls, trickling a spoonful of cream into each bowl. Sprinkle with parsley.

Serves 6-8

Ginger and Carrot Soup

Ginger and lime give an intriguing and delicate flavor to this versatile soup, which may be eaten cold or warm.

1 tablespoon ginger root, chopped
2 cloves garlic, minced
1 medium onion, chopped
2 tablespoons butter
5-6 large carrots (about 2 lbs or 1 kg), sliced
30 oz (900 ml or 1½ pints or 4 cups) chicken broth
juice of a fresh small lime
salt and freshly ground fresh pepper
yogurt or crème fraîche for garnish
snipped fresh chives for garnish

1. In a large pot, sauté ginger, garlic, and onion in butter until tender. Stir in carrots.
2. Add chicken broth and water and simmer until carrots are tender, about 20-25 minutes.
3. Add lime juice and salt and pepper.
4. Purée soup in a food processor or blender until smooth. Add more broth if needed.
5. Chill to serve cold. Or reheat gently and serve hot.
6. Garnish each soup bowl of soup with a dollop of yogurt or crème fraîche and chives.

Serves 8-10

Shredded Carrot Appetizer

This crisp, tasty, and refreshing salad could make part of an hors d'oeuvre selection or accompany a main dish in place of a green salad. It may be varied with the addition of two crushed garlic cloves. Or add a teaspoon of ground cumin to give it a Moroccan tang.

1 lb (450 g) or 4 medium carrots
juice of 1 lemon
juice of 1 orange
4 oz (100 g or ½ cup) dried currants (optional)
3 tablespoons olive oil
3 tablespoons chopped fresh parsley, coriander, or mint
salt and freshly ground black pepper to taste

1. Shred carrots coarsely using a food processor and place in a salad bowl.
2. Toss together with remaining ingredients.
3. Cover and refrigerate. Serve cold.

Serves 4-6

Herbed Carrot Salad

Other fresh herbs may be substituted for the parsley and dill.

6 medium carrots, cut in ¼ inch (.6 cm) slices
3 tablespoons olive oil
2 tablespoons fresh lemon juice
¼ teaspoon pepper
1 clove garlic, minced (optional)
2 tablespoons chopped fresh parsley
2 tablespoons chopped fresh dill

1. Cook the carrots in boiling water until they are tender, about 10 minutes. Drain.
2. Beat the oil, lemon juice, minced garlic and pepper together with a whisk. Pour mixture over carrots.
3. Add parsley and dill. Chill before serving.

Serves 4-6

Oriental Carrot Salad

Sesame oil gives the unexpected and delightful flavor to this salad.

3 medium carrots, shredded
half a small green pepper, finely minced
2 teaspoons sesame oil
2 teaspoons vegetable oil
juice of half a lemon
1 tablespoon soy sauce
1/8 teaspoon ground ginger
1 teaspoon brown sugar
dash garlic powder
1 tablespoon toasted sesame seeds

1. Combine the shredded carrots and minced green pepper in a medium bowl.
2. Blend remaining ingredients together in a small bowl and add to carrot mixture, blending all together well.
3. Chill several hours before serving.

Note: To toast sesame seeds, place them in a shallow pan in a 350°F (180°C) oven for 15 minutes or until lightly toasted, stirring occasionally.

Serves 4

Asian Carrot and Cabbage Salad

*This nice variation on an oriental-style salad makes another
pleasant change from simple green salads.*

2 carrots, peeled and grated
1 lb (450 g) cabbage, cored and shredded
2-3 spring onions, finely chopped
2-3 oz (60-90 ml) peanut or vegetable oil
2 tablespoons fresh lime juice
1 teaspoon soy sauce
salt and pepper to taste

1. Place prepared vegetables in a salad bowl.
2. Combine the oil, lime juice and soy sauce and whisk together.
   Add salt and pepper if you want to.
3. Add dressing to the vegetables, toss, and serve.

Serves 4

Carrots in Raspberry Vinegar

The tart and spicy flavor of this unusual accompaniment improves when kept refrigerated for several days.

1½ lbs (750 g) carrots
4 fl oz (100 ml or ½ cup) raspberry vinegar
4 fl oz (100 ml or ½ cup) olive oil
freshly ground black pepper

1. Peel the carrots and cut them into slices 1/8 inch (1/2 cm) thick.
2. Place them in a pot of boiling salted water and cook for about 6 minutes, until nearly tender but still crisp.
3. Drain and place carrots in a bowl. Sprinkle with raspberry vinegar while they are still hot.
4. Add olive oil and mix well.
5. Refrigerate overnight or longer.
6. When ready to serve, return carrots to room temperature, and remove them from the marinade with a slotted spoon, allowing some remaining liquid to cling to the carrots. Sprinkle with black pepper to taste.

Serves 6

Buttered Carrots

Cooking young carrots in a buttery glaze retains the full flavor of the tender young carrots and makes a simple but delicious side dish.

3-4 carrots (about 1 lb or 500 g), sliced thin or cut into sticks
2 tablespoons butter
salt and pepper
2 fl oz (50 ml or ¼ cup) water
chopped parsley, mint, or dill

1. Peel carrots and cut them into thin slices or sticks.
2. Melt the butter in a saucepan over low heat, add carrots and season with salt and freshly ground black pepper. Coat carrots evenly with butter, taking care not to brown them.
3. Add a small amount of water, just enough to cover the carrots, and bring to a boil. Cover pan and simmer gently for 15-20 minutes until tender.
4. Remove the lid, raise the heat and cook carrots until liquid evaporates and only butter remains, making sure carrots do not brown.
5. Mix parsley, dill, or mint in with the carrots and turn into a hot serving dish.

Serves 4-6

Carrots and Leeks

Leeks combine well with carrots.

4 medium-large carrots, sliced
1 leek, carefully cleaned and cut into slices
1 tablespoon olive oil
¼ teaspoon thyme

1. Cut carrots into thin slices.
2. Sauté sliced leek in olive oil until tender. Add carrots and thyme.
3. Cover and cook over low heat until carrots are tender.

Serves 4-6

Carrots and Chicory

Sweet carrots and bitter chicory complement each other and make an excellent accompaniment, especially with chicken or veal. This dish can also be transferred to a casserole and heated in a moderate oven before serving.

small onion, chopped
1 tablespoon butter
3-4 medium carrots, cut into rings
2 chicory, cut into rings
freshly ground black pepper

1. Fry onion in butter over low heat in a covered saucepan until golden. Place carrot rings over the onions. Cover and simmer for 20 minutes, stirring occasionally.
2. Add chicory rings, and simmer until tender. Sprinkle with pepper and transfer to a serving dish.
3. Alternatively, transfer to a casserole and heat in oven.

Serves 4-6

Carrots Vinaigrette

This is an enticing cold vegetable choice for a buffet or barbecue dinner. And it uses a lot of carrots!

12 carrots, cut into strips
3 tablespoons oil
2 tablespoons green pepper, chopped
1½ tablespoons cider vinegar
1 tablespoon pickle relish
1 tablespoon lemon juice
1 teaspoon paprika
½ teaspoon dry mustard
½ teaspoon garlic powder
½ teaspoon salt
¼ teaspoon basil leaves
freshly ground black pepper to taste

1. Cut the carrots into julienne strips and steam 1-2 minutes until tender but still crisp.
2. Combine remaining ingredients to make vinaigrette sauce, and pour sauce over cooked carrots.
3. Refrigerate for at least an hour and serve cold.

Serves 8

Ginger Carrots

This sweet and spicy carrot dish, welcome any time of the year, can be prepared in advance by simply stopping before the last step. When ready to serve, cook over low heat, then transfer to a serving dish.

12 medium-size carrots, cut into 1-inch (2.5 cm) strips
4 tablespoons butter
6 tablespoons brown sugar
1½ teaspoons ground ginger
½ teaspoon caraway seeds

1. Place carrots in a pot with enough cold water to cover. Cook 20 to 25 minutes or until tender.
2. In a small saucepan, melt butter and add brown sugar, ginger, and caraway seeds. Blend the mixture together.
3. Drain the cooked carrots and return them to the pot. Pour the butter mixture over the carrots and cook, stirring occasionally, over low heat for 5 minutes.
4. Turn out into a vegetable dish and serve.

Serves 6-8

Roast Tamari Carrots

Tamari is a Japanese soy sauce that is wheat free, light and elegant, and less salty than other types. Its nutty and fermented soybean flavor adds a touch of the East as it enlarges and enlivens your carrot repertoire.

1 lb carrots (450 g), thickly sliced (or whole baby carrots)
1 tablespoon tamari
1 tablespoon olive oil
freshly ground black pepper
½ tablespoon honey (optional)
parsley for garnish

1. Whisk together in a bowl the tamari, olive oil, and black pepper. Toss the mixture with the carrots until they are well coated.
2. Arrange carrot slices in a baking dish and bake in an oven preheated at 400°F (200°C) for about 30 minutes or until tender and nicely browned. You can insure browning by sprinkling with a tablespoon of honey near the end of cooking time.
3. Sprinkle with chopped fresh parsley and serve.

Serves 4

Baked Carrot Sticks

As this recipe illustrates, carrots can be very successfully baked in the oven. At the same time, it can alleviate last-minute rush while the carrots busily bake, leaving you free to busily deal with other preparations.

2 lbs (900 g) carrots, peeled and cut into sticks
1 teaspoon salt
1 teaspoon brown sugar
freshly ground black pepper or dash cinnamon
3 tablespoons butter

1. Place carrots in a shallow casserole or baking dish. Sprinkle with salt, sugar, and either pepper or cinnamon, depending on your preference. Mix together and dot with butter.
2. Cover and bake in preheated oven at 350°F (180°C) for about 45-50 minutes, stopping halfway through to stir the mixture.

Serves 8

Orange Honey Carrots

This is another quick way to turn carrots into a delectable dish to serve for company.

6 medium carrots, sliced
juice of 1 orange
1 tablespoon grated orange rind
1 tablespoon honey
1 tablespoon butter

1. Cook the carrots in boiling water until tender, about 10-15 minutes. Drain.
2. Add the other ingredients. Heat through and serve.

Serves 6

Honeyed Carrot and Apple Bake

With its sweet blend of carrots and apples, this simple-to-make recipe will turn a meal into something special.

3-4 medium carrots (about 1 lb or 450 g), coarsely shredded
2 small apples, peeled and coarsely shredded
½ teaspoon ground cinnamon
1 tablespoon honey
2 fl oz (50 ml or ¼ cup) orange juice
1 tablespoon wheat germ
¼ teaspoon ground cinnamon
2 teaspoons butter

1. In a large bowl, combine shredded carrots and apples with cinnamon, honey, and orange juice. Mix well.
2. Turn mixture into a lightly-oiled baking dish and press it down gently.
3. For the topping, mix wheat germ and cinnamon together and sprinkle evenly over the carrots. Dot with butter.
4. Bake uncovered in oven preheated to 350°F (180°C) for 40 minutes. Serve hot.

Serves 4

Carrot Tzimmes

This festive dish is especially easy because it can be prepared ahead of time and simply heated when ready to serve.

1½ lbs (750 g) carrots, cut in ¼-inch (.6 cm) slices
14 oz (375 g or 1½ cups) pitted prunes or apricots or a
  combination of both
juice of 1 orange
2 tablespoons honey
¼ teaspoon ground ginger (optional)

1. Cook carrots in boiling water until tender, about 15 minutes. Drain and transfer to a casserole.
2. Place dried fruit in water in another saucepan and bring to a boil, then simmer covered for 15 minutes. Drain and reserve the cooking liquid. Combine the fruit and carrots.
3. Mix the orange juice together with the honey, 2 tablespoons of the cooked fruit liquid, and ginger (if wanted). Pour over the carrots and fruit.
4. Heat in a 350°F (180°C) oven for 15 minutes.

Serves 6-8

Sweet and Sour Carrots

Serve this vegetable dish either hot or cold.

1 lb (450 g) carrots, sliced diagonally
1 medium green pepper, cut into bite-sized pieces
1 tin (8 oz or 125 g) pineapple chunks (with its own juice)
2 oz (50 g or ¼ cup) sugar
1 tablespoon cornflour (cornstarch)
½ teaspoon salt
2 tablespoons cider vinegar
1 teaspoon soy sauce

1. Cook carrots for about 10 minutes, or until tender. Add green pepper and cook another 3 minutes. Drain and set aside.
2. Drain pineapple juice into a cup and add enough water to measure 3 fl oz (90 ml or 1/3 cup) liquid. Reserve pineapple chunks.
3. In a small saucepan, combine sugar, cornflour and salt. Add pineapple liquid, vinegar and soy sauce and stir until smooth. Bring to a boil while stirring over medium heat. Then simmer for 1-2 minutes until thickened.
4. Pour sauce over carrots and green pepper. Stir in pineapple and serve hot. Or chill to serve cold.

Serves 6

Spiced Cider Carrots

The natural sweetness of this colorful vegetable is enhanced by the cider and given an extra tang by the mustard and rosemary.

1 lb (450 g) carrots, diced
1 oz (25 g) butter
3 fl oz (75 ml) cider
3 fl oz (75 ml) water
2 teaspoons fresh chopped rosemary or 1 teaspoon dried
1 teaspoon mustard powder

1. Melt the butter in a saucepan. Add diced carrots and cook over gentle heat for 5 minutes.
2. Pour in the cider and water. Add the rosemary and mustard and mix together.
3. Bring to a boil, then simmer, covered, for 10 minutes, making certain there is enough liquid.
4. When carrots are tender, place them in a hot serving dish. Boil remaining liquid until it makes a thick and syrupy glaze. Pour this over the top and serve.

Serves 4

Turkish Fried Carrots

*Yogurt is used as a dressing for this recipe, which goes
particularly well with lamb.*

1½ lbs (750 g) carrots
salt and black pepper
1 tablespoon seasoned flour
2 tablespoons olive oil
½ pint (10 oz or 300 g) natural yogurt
1 tablespoon chopped mint

1. Peel and wash the carrots. Cut into ¼ inch (.6 cm) slices.
2. Boil water in a saucepan; cook carrots for about 10 minutes, until nearly tender. Drain them in a colander, and spread them on paper towels to dry thoroughly.
3. Toss the carrots in flour seasoned with pepper. Heat the oil in a pan and fry the carrots over medium heat until golden brown. Season to taste with salt and freshly ground pepper.
4. Place the yogurt in a pan and warm it over low heat. Do not let it boil or it will curdle.
5. Turn carrots into a hot serving dish. Pour yogurt over it, and garnish with mint.

Serves 4-6

Carrots Vichy

Perhaps this flavorful recipe emanated from Vichy, but fortunately it has traveled away from its source.

10 medium carrots, sliced
5 fl oz (150 ml or 2/3 cup) chicken broth
2 tablespoons butter
1 tablespoon sugar
pinch of salt
2 tablespoons chopped fresh parsley

1. Peel and slice the carrots.
2. Combine broth, butter, sugar, and salt in a saucepan. Add the carrots and simmer, covered, until broth cooks away.
3. Shake pan over low heat or stir gently until carrot slices are glazed. Sprinkle with parsley before serving.

Serves 6-8

Hunter Style Carrots

The name of this recipe is appropriate because it goes so well with any strong meat or lamb, or with duck or goose.

½ oz (12 g) dried wild mushrooms
8 fl oz (200 ml or ½ cup) Madeira wine
3 tablespoons olive oil
1½ lbs (700 g) thin carrots, sliced diagonally
2 large cloves garlic, chopped
3 tablespoons fresh flat-leaf parsley
salt and freshly ground black pepper

1. Soak the washed mushrooms in the Madeira for 2 hours. Drain them, setting aside any remaining liquid. Chop mushrooms and set them aside.
2. Heat oil in a large frying pan, and sauté the carrots in the oil over medium heat for about 10 minutes, stirring from time to time.
3. Add the chopped mushrooms and any remaining Madeira wine. Continue to sauté for about another 10 minutes, stirring until the carrots start browning.
4. Mix in the garlic and parsley. Sprinkle with salt and pepper, and transfer to a heated serving dish.

Serves 6

Carrot and Potato Pudding

Here is a dish that combines earthy potatoes and sweet carrots to make a luscious addition to any meal.

4 medium carrots (1 lb or 450 g), finely shredded
2 medium potatoes (12 oz or 325 g), finely shredded
6 tablespoons brown sugar
3 tablespoons butter, melted
1 teaspoon ground cinnamon
1 teaspoon ground nutmeg
1 teaspoon baking soda
8 tablespoons flour

1. Combine all ingredients in a large bowl and mix well. Turn into an oiled baking dish and press mixture down with the back of a spoon.
2. Cover and bake in an oven preheated to 350°F (180°C) for 30 minutes. Uncover and continue baking 30 minutes more.

Serves 6

Carrot Pudding Mold

To make an even more attractive presentation, heap a cooked green vegetable into the center of the mold.

2 lbs (1 kg) carrots, sliced
2 medium onions, chopped
32 fl oz (1 litre or 4 cups) chicken broth
1½ teaspoons salt
6 eggs
6 oz (175 g) matzo meal

1. Place sliced carrots and chopped onions in a saucepan. Add the broth, cover and bring to a boil, then simmer over low heat until tender.
2. Drain onions and carrots, setting aside the cooking liquid.
3. Purée vegetables in a food processor.
4. Add the eggs and matzo meal, and process for another 2 or 3 seconds. Gradually add enough of the reserved liquid to make a nice thick consistency.
5. Pour mixture into a well-buttered ring mold. Bake in an oven preheated to 375°F (190°C) for 45 minutes or until firm. Unmold onto a platter and serve hot.

Serves 6-8

Note: You can make the required amount of matzo meal by placing 3 matzos, broken in pieces, in food processor and whirling until a coarse meal is obtained.

Carrot Kugel

Another exquisite way to enjoy carrots.

6 oz (170 g or 1¼ cups) flour
¾ teaspoon salt
1½ teaspoons baking powder
1 teaspoon baking soda
1 teaspoon cinnamon
¼ teaspoon ginger
¼ teaspoon nutmeg
¼ teaspoon cloves
6 fl oz (175 ml or ¾ cup) oil
4 oz (100 g or ½ cup) brown sugar
1 egg
1 tablespoon water
1 tablespoon lemon juice
4 medium carrots, grated

1. Stir together all the dry ingredients except sugar.
2. Beat the oil, brown sugar and egg. Stir in the flour mixture.
3. Stir in the water, lemon juice, and grated carrots. Mix well.
4. Turn into a greased 8-inch (20 cm) baking dish and bake in a 350°F (180°C) oven for 35 minutes.

Serves 6-8

Carrot Curry

Serve this main-course vegetarian Indian curry over rice with a sweet chutney.

4 tablespoons butter
3-4 cloves garlic, crushed
1 teaspoon fresh ginger, minced
1 teaspoon mustard seeds
1 teaspoon ground cumin
1 teaspoon ground coriander
1 teaspoon dill weed
1 teaspoon turmeric
2 small red onions, sliced
1½ teaspoons salt
2 small potatoes, cut into thin slices
4 large carrots, cut into thin slices
16 fl oz (450 ml or 2 cups) orange juice
cayenne pepper, to taste
2 red bell peppers, cut into thin slices
10 oz (275 g) toasted cashew pieces
8 oz (225 g or 1 cup) yogurt

1. Melt the butter in a deep frying pan. Add the garlic, ginger, and mustard seeds. Sauté over medium heat for about 3-5 minutes, until the seeds begin to pop.
2. Stir in the remaining spices and the onions, salt, potatoes, and carrots. Continue stirring for another 5-8 minutes. Add the orange juice. Cover and simmer for about 10-15 minutes, until the potatoes are tender.
3. Add the cayenne, the red pepper slices, and the cashews. Cover and allow to cook another few minutes, until the peppers are just barely done.
4. Stir the yogurt into the hot curry just before serving.

Serves 4

Carrot Chutney

This northern India chutney that comes from Bengal is a condiment that can also be used with non-Indian dishes.

8 oz (225 g) carrots, peeled and sliced
1 onion, peeled and sliced
1 lb (450 g) apples, cored and sliced
4 oz (100 g) raisins
4 oz (100 g) freshly grated horseradish
8 oz (225 g) brown sugar
2 teaspoons salt
3 teaspoons ground ginger
3 teaspoons curry powder
1 teaspoon mustard seeds
1½ tablespoons golden syrup
10 fl oz (300 ml) vinegar

1. Place the sliced carrots, onions, and apples in a saucepan. Add all the remaining ingredients.
2. Simmer, stirring occasionally, for about 50 minutes, or until mixture has thickened.
3. Fill sterilized jars with the chutney up to 1/8 inch (.3 cm) from the tops. Seal and keep them in a cool dark place. Allow to stand for 6 weeks before using so that flavors will develop.

Makes 2½ lbs or 1.15 kg

Carrot Jam

Brandy gives this unusual jam an extra kick. But note that jam must have pectin, found in most fruits, in order to set. Liquid pectin, or preserving sugar with pectin added, will insure a good set.

2 lbs (1 kg) carrots, peeled and coarsely chopped
30 oz (900 ml) water
24 oz (1½ lbs or 675 g) preserving sugar
2 large lemons, grated rind and juice
3 teaspoons ginger, freshly grated
1½ tablespoons brandy

1. Place the chopped carrots in a large pot with the water and bring to a boil. Lower heat and simmer with lid on for 20 minutes. When carrots are soft, purée them in a food processor or blender.
2. Return puréed mixture to pot. Add sugar, finely grated lemon rind and lemon juice, and grated ginger. Stir over low heat until sugar is dissolved.
3. Raise the heat and boil rapidly without stirring for 15-20 minutes, until it is at setting point.
4. Remove from heat. You can test whether it has reached setting point by using a sugar thermometer which should read 220°F (104°C).
5. Skim off any scum from the top, mix in the brandy, and pour jam into sterilized jars to within 1/8 inch (.3 cm) of the tops. Seal.

Makes about 1¼ lbs (575 g)

Carrot Soufflé

This elegant dessert can be prepared and refrigerated a day or two before your dinner party.

8 oz (225 g or 1 cup) sugar (or less)
6 eggs, separated
1 lb (450 g or 1 cup) carrots, cooked and mashed
2 tablespoons orange juice
1 tablespoon lemon juice
6 oz (175 g) blanched almonds, grated
raspberry jam
8 fl oz (225 ml or 1 cup) heavy cream, whipped

1. Mix sugar together with 6 egg yolks. Blend in the carrots, orange juice, lemon juice, and grated almonds.
2. Fold in 6 egg whites, stiffly beaten.
3. Pour mixture into soufflé dish and bake at 350°F (180°C) for 45 minutes.
4. When cool, spread a layer of raspberry jam over it.
5. Cover with whipped cream.

Serves 8

Golden Carrot Bread

Heavily spiced with cinnamon, this loaf has a rich color and close texture. It freezes well or will keep for several days in an air-tight container.

4 fl oz (100 ml or ½ cup) orange juice
3 fl oz (75 ml or 1/3 cup) sunflower oil
6 tablespoons sugar
1 egg
2 teaspoons vanilla
5 oz (140 g or 1 cup) whole wheat or whole meal flour
5 oz (140 g or 1 cup) all-purpose flour
1 tablespoon cinnamon
1 teaspoon baking powder
½ teaspoon baking soda
¼ teaspoon salt
2 medium carrots, grated

1. Combine orange juice, oil, sugar, egg and vanilla in a large bowl and beat together.
2. Add dry ingredients to orange juice mixture and blend. Beat in grated carrots.
3. Turn into a lightly greased 9x5-inch (23x12 cm) loaf pan and bake in an oven preheated to 350°F (180°C) for about 40 minutes.

Carrot-Oatmeal Muffins

*These muffins are not for breakfast only. They go well with soup
or salad or a light dish. They are easy to make, call for
ingredients that are probably available at home, and take only
twenty minutes to bake.*

3 oz (75 g) butter, softened
1 egg
5 oz (150 g or about ¾ cup) brown sugar
6 fl oz (175 ml or ¾ cup) milk
2 medium carrots (about 1 cup), finely grated
4 oz (110 g or 1 cup) oatmeal
6½ oz (180 g or 1¼ cups) flour
2½ teaspoons baking powder
½ teaspoon salt
½ teaspoon allspice or cinnamon
3 oz (75 g or 2/3 cup) raisins (optional)

1. Beat the butter, egg, and brown sugar together until you have
   a smooth mixture.
2. Stir in the milk, carrot and oatmeal.
3. Add sifted flour to this mixture together with baking powder,
   salt and allspice. Mix in the raisins if desired.
4. Turn into a greased muffin pan and bake in oven preheated to
   400°F (200°C) for about 20 minutes.

Makes one dozen muffins

Mediterranean Carrot Cake

Your guests will love this one!

4 eggs, separated
8 oz (225g) sugar
grated rind of a lemon
8 oz (225 g) carrots, finely grated
8 oz (225g) grated almonds
1 heaping tablespoon flour
1/8 teaspoon baking powder
pine kernels (optional)
icing sugar
crème fraîche (optional)

1. Beat the egg yolks, sugar and lemon rind together very thoroughly. Mix in the carrots, almonds, flour, and baking powder.
2. Beat the egg whites until they form a stiff peak and gently fold them into the mixture.
3. Spoon the cake mixture into a well-buttered 8-inch (20 cm) spring form pan. Sprinkle a heaping tablespoon of pine kernels over the top.
4. Bake at 350°F (180°C) for about 50 minutes.
5. Before serving, sprinkle with icing (confectioner's) sugar. Serve topped with a spoonful of crème fraîche if you want to.

Serves 6-8

Easy and Elegant Carrot Cake

This recipe makes a splendid birthday cake or dinner party dessert. It is best made the day before you want to use it and also freezes well for weeks without the icing.

6 oz (175 g or 1¼ cups) plain flour, sifted
1 teaspoon baking powder
1 teaspoon baking soda
1 teaspoon ground cinnamon
¼ teaspoon salt
10 fl oz (300 ml or 1¼ cups) sunflower oil
10 oz (280 g or 1¼ cups) sugar
3 large eggs
2 medium carrots (about 8 oz or 225g) grated

Filling and icing:
6 oz (175 g) cream cheese
6 oz (175 g) butter
8 oz (225 g) icing or confectioner's sugar
½ teaspoon vanilla

1. Sift the dry ingredients together.
2. Place oil in a large bowl with the sugar and beat together. Add eggs, one at a time, beating well after each addition. Fold in the dry ingredients and mix well. Stir in the grated carrot.
3. Transfer the mixture to a greased 10-inch (25 cm) round cake tin and bake in a moderate oven at 350°F (180°C) for 45 minutes. Then lower the heat to 325°F (170°C) and bake for an additional 20 minutes. Cake is done when skewer inserted into the center comes out clean. Allow to stand for 5 minutes, then turn out onto a rack and cool before you make the filling.

4. For the filling, beat together the cream cheese and butter and gradually add the icing sugar, sifting as you add it. Beat thoroughly, adding the vanilla.
5. Cover top and sides with the icing. Alternatively, you can split the cake in half and spread the butter cream icing between the layers and over top and sides.

Serves 8-10

Carrot Cookies

Great for the lunch box or for a snack.

2 medium carrots
6 oz (175 g) butter
4 oz (110 g) sugar
1 egg
rind of ¼ medium orange, minced
12 oz (340 g or 2¼ cups) all-purpose flour
2 teaspoons baking powder
½ teaspoon salt
1/8 teaspoon ground allspice
1/8 teaspoon ground nutmeg
4 oz (100 g or 1 cup) walnuts, chopped
4 oz (100 g) currants or raisins

1. Grate carrots and set aside.
2. Cream butter and sugar together in a large bowl.
3. Add grated carrots to the creamed mixture along with the egg and orange rind. Mix all the ingredients together.
4. In another bowl combine sifted flour, baking powder, salt, and spices. Add to carrot mixture and beat until well mixed.
5. Add walnuts and currants or raisins and stir well.
6. Drop dough by spoonfuls onto a well-greased baking sheet. Bake in an oven preheated to 375°F (190°C) for about 10-12 minutes or until lightly browned around the edges. Remove from oven, loosen around the edges and set on a rack to cool.

Makes about 3 dozen

Celeriac

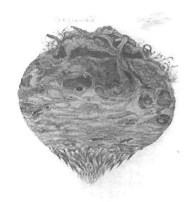

CELERIAC

If vegetables can be said to be subject to the rules of fashion, this one has become quite fashionable. Developed in Renaissance times, celeriac did not make it to Britain until 1723 when a gardener introduced it using seeds coming from Alexandria. Finally, it is now coming into its own.

Celeriac, sometimes called celery root, is a winter root vegetable that is in season from October to March. It is a turnip-shaped and knobbly tuber that varies in size and has a brown fibrous skin. Despite its unattractive appearance, this bulbous root continues to gain in popularity because of its appeal to the palate. Its white flesh, the texture of a turnip or swede, is reminiscent of a strong celery flavor with a nutty sweetness and subtle aniseed taste. Much easier to grow than celery, and with a more pungent and intense flavor, celeriac makes a desirable and delicious root vegetable.

Its many uses include boiling (for 25-30 minutes) or steaming (35 minutes), frying strips in butter (30 minutes), puréeing, or grating fresh as a salad. When grated and eaten raw, as in salads, it has a crunchy texture, but it is more akin to potatoes when cooked. For best flavor, celeriac should be hard, firm, and crisp with no soft spots.

To prepare celeriac, cut off top and bottom and place the flat base securely on a cutting board. Use a sharp knife to cut around the sides to remove the outer layer.

After it is peeled and sliced, diced or grated, place it in a bowl of acidulated water (water with lemon juice or vinegar added) as the flesh discolors when exposed to light and air. So, if used in a salad, give it an instant dressing with lemon juice or vinegar.

RECIPES for CELERIAC

Celeriac and Celery Soup with Roquefort Croutons

Friends who say they don't like the taste of celery nevertheless love this soup.

1 tablespoon butter
1 large leek, thinly sliced
2-3 small shallots, chopped
2 medium celeriac, peeled and chopped
2 potatoes, peeled and cubed
8 fl oz (225 ml or 1 cup) water
28 fl oz (825 ml) chicken broth
2 thyme sprigs
2 bay leaves
2 celery stalks, thinly sliced
8 fl oz (225 ml or 1 cup) milk
½ teaspoon salt
½ teaspoon freshly ground black pepper
2 oz (50 ml or ¼ cup) light cream

for croutons (optional):
8 slices (½ inch or 1.2 cm thick) French bread baguette
2 oz (50-60 g or ½ cup) crumbled Roquefort cheese

1. Melt butter in a pot over medium heat. Add leek and shallots and cook until tender, about 5 minutes, stirring frequently. Add celeriac, potato, water, broth, thyme, and bay leaves. Bring to a boil, then reduce heat, cover and simmer until vegetables are tender, about 15 minutes.
2. Stir in celery, milk, salt and pepper. Simmer 10 minutes but do not allow to boil. Remove from heat and allow to stand for 5 minutes. Discard bay leaves and thyme.
3. Blend the mixture in a food processor until smooth. Stir in cream.

4. Prepare croutons by arranging 8 French baguette slices on a baking sheet. Broil 1 minute or until golden. Turn each slice over, sprinkle with Roquefort cheese, and broil another minute or until cheese melts. Cut each slice of bread into 6 wedges.
5. Ladle soup into bowls and top each serving with 6 croutons. Serve immediately.

Serves 8

Celeriac and Orange Soup

Other root vegetables can be substituted for the celeriac.

4 oz (100 g) butter
1 medium-large onion, finely chopped
2 lbs (900 g) prepared celeriac
2-3 fl oz (50-75 ml) sherry (optional)
35 fl oz (1 litre) chicken or beef stock
juice and rind of 2 oranges
fresh mint leaves (optional)

1. Sauté onions in butter until tender. Add cut-up celeriac pieces and continue cooking until tender.
2. Add orange juice and grated orange rind and mix together.
3. Add sherry (if you want to) and stock and continue cooking about 30 minutes or until vegetables are tender.
4. Remove from heat. Blend in food processor until desired consistency is reached.
5. When ready to serve, garnish with mint leaves.

Serves 6-8

Celeriac Salad

This salad of raw celeriac can be served on its own or with thinly sliced salami or Parma ham.

1 large celeriac
2-3 tablespoons mayonnaise
¼ teaspoon French mustard
lemon juice

1. Peel the celeriac and cut into thin matchstick strips.
2. Blend the mayonnaise and mustard and season to taste with lemon juice.
3. Toss the celeriac thoroughly in the dressing and allow to stand in the refrigerator until ready to serve.

Serves 4

Piquant Celeriac Salad

Celeriac, fast becoming a popular vegetable, is the basis for a winter salad that could become as popular as it is pleasing.

2 celeriac knobs
1 tablespoon finely chopped onion
4 fl oz (100 ml or ½ cup) olive oil
3 tablespoons lemon juice
1 tablespoon chopped parsley
salt and freshly ground black pepper
mayonnaise (optional)

1. Cook celeriac in boiling water, covered, until tender, about 25 minutes. Cool, peel, and cut into thin strips.
2. In a large bowl, blend the onion, oil, lemon juice, parsley, salt and pepper. Add the celeriac strips and mix together.
3. Marinate overnight in the refrigerator. Serve garnished with mayonnaise, if you want to.

Serves 6

Curried Celeriac Salad with Dried Cherries

This colorful and exotic salad makes a welcome change—and you can substitute dried cranberries for the cherries.

2 oz (56 g or ½ cup) dried tart cherries
1 small (or half a large) red onion, finely chopped
3 tablespoons plain yogurt
3 tablespoons sour cream
1 tablespoon Dijon mustard
1 teaspoon curry powder
1 teaspoon olive oil
½ teaspoon sugar
½ teaspoon salt
1 lb (450 g) celeriac, peeled and shredded

1. Combine all ingredients except celeriac in a large bowl, and stir with a whisk.
2. Add celeriac and toss well to coat. Cover and chill for at least 2 hours.

Serves 4

Celeriac, Mushroom and Bacon Salad

Here is another salad to augment your celeriac repertoire.

6 oz (175g) celeriac
4 oz (125 g) mushrooms, sliced
4 oz (125 g) bacon
2-3 sprigs parsley, chopped
3 tablespoons yogurt
1 tablespoon lemon juice
1 tablespoon sunflower oil
1 teaspoon French mustard
salt and freshly ground black pepper to taste

1. Peel and grate the celeriac. Place in a salad bowl with sliced mushrooms.
2. Chop the fried or grilled bacon and add to vegetables.
3. Blend remaining ingredients thoroughly and pour this dressing over the salad. Toss well and serve.

Serves 6

Roasted Celeriac and Root Vegetables

Just as celeriac has become fashionable, so are oven-cooked vegetables in fashion, and this recipe may present an easy opportunity to try a vegetable that is new to you or your family.

2 lbs (900 g) celeriac or celery root
1 lb (450 g) swedes or rutabaga
1 lb (450 g) carrots
1 tablespoon olive oil
1 large red onion, cut into 1-inch pieces
1 teaspoon ground sage
1 teaspoon salt

1. Peel the celeriac and cut into ½ x 2-inch (1.2 x 5 cm) strips. Peel the swedes and cut into strips of the same size.
2. In a large bowl, combine both with baby carrots or carrots cut into strips. Add olive oil and toss to coat the vegetables. Turn the vegetable mixture into a shallow baking dish.
3. Roast for 25 minutes in an oven preheated to 400°F (200°C). Then stir in the red onion, sage and salt, and roast for an additional 25 minutes, stirring occasionally, until all the vegetables are tender and golden.

Serves 8

Celeriac and Potato Purée

*The distinct flavor of celeriac combines well with other root
vegetables such as potatoes. This purée goes particularly well
with game.*

1 lb (450 g) celeriac or 1 large one
1 lb (450 g) potatoes
3 tablespoons butter
salt and freshly ground black pepper to taste
4 fl oz (100 ml or ½ cup) cream or milk
chopped parsley leaves for garnish

1. Peel the celeriac and the potatoes and cut into pieces about 1-2
   inches (2.5-5 cm) in diameter. Cook in boiling water for about
   15-20 minutes or until tender, being careful not to overcook.
   As the potatoes take less time, cook the two vegetables
   separately.
2. Drain well. Mash the vegetables with the butter, then purée
   them in a blender or food processor. Add cream to make a
   smooth consistency.
3. Season with salt and pepper and blend it all together. Turn into
   a serving bowl or casserole.
4. Heat thoroughly over low heat when ready. Sprinkle with
   parsley and serve.

Serves 4-6

Celeriac and Sweet Potato Mash

*Rena, the superb hostess who gave me this recipe—with
measurements to be determined by the cook—prepares this in
advance and reheats when required.*

celeriac
sweet potato
pepper to taste
cream, crème fraîch or mascarpone

1. Boil together equal quantities of celeriac and sweet potato.
   Drain, making sure you extract as much water as possible.
2. Mash the vegetables together with pepper and either cream or
   crème fraîche, or mascarpone.
3. Spoon into a casserole and serve, or reheat when ready.

Celeriac Gratin

In this dish, the sweet and nutty flavour of celeriac is enhanced by the Emmental cheese.

**1 lb (450 g) celeriac, peeled and cut into ¼ inch (.6 cm) slices
juice of 1 lemon
1 oz (25 g) butter
1 small onion, chopped
2 tablespoons flour
10 fl oz (300 ml or 1¼ cups) milk
1 oz (25 g) Emmental cheese, grated
1 tablespoon capers (optional)
salt and cayenne pepper**

1. Place prepared celeriac in a saucepan of cold water acidulated with the lemon juice.
2. Bring to a boil, then simmer celeriac until tender, about 10 minutes. Drain and arrange celeriac slices in a baking dish.
3. In a saucepan, melt the butter and sauté finely chopped onion until soft. Stir in the flour and cook for 1 minute. Then stir in the milk slowly until you have a smooth sauce.
4. Stir in the cheese, capers and seasonings. Pour the mixture over the celeriac.
5. Bake in oven preheated to 375°F (190°C) until top is golden brown, about 15-20 minutes.

Serves 4

Celeriac Croquettes

Celeriac, a stylish vegetable, can also be made into tasty croquettes.

1½ lbs (700 g) celeriac
2 eggs
pinch of freshly grated nutmeg
2 tablespoons minced fresh parsley leaves
2 oz (50-60 g or ½ cup) freshly grated Parmesan cheese
salt and pepper to taste
flour (if needed)
olive oil or butter as needed
plain bread crumbs as needed

1. Peel the celeriac and cut into pieces. Place in pot of boiling water to cover and cook until tender, about 15 minutes. Drain and mash.
2. Mix the mashed celeriac with eggs, nutmeg, parsley, Parmesan cheese, salt and pepper. Add only enough flour (you may not need any) to help celeriac hold its shape as you form it into cakes. Refrigerate for 1 hour.
3. Place oil or butter in frying pan on medium-high. Dredge the cakes in bread crumbs and place them in the pan for about 5 minutes, until brown on one side, then turn over and brown the other side.
4. Garnish with more parsley (if you want to) and serve.

Serves 4-6

Celeriac Chips

These startlingly good chips will surprise dinner guests.

2 or 3 celeriacs
vegetable oil
salt

1. Peel celeriac and cut into strips the shape of chips or French fried potatoes.
2. Heat oil in a large roasting or frying pan and sear the celeriac pieces. Sprinkle with salt. Allow to brown around the edges. Toss gently a few times to obtain an even golden color.
3. Place roasting pan filled with the lightly browned chips in a preheated oven at 350°F (180°C) for about 30 minutes, tossing from time to time for an even color. Serve.

Serves 6-8

Jerusalem Artichokes

JERUSALEM ARTICHOKES

These ginger-like tubers have nothing to do with Jerusalem or artichokes. The name is a seventeenth-century corruption of the Italian, *girasole articiocco*, because its flowers turn with the sun and look like sunflowers and its taste is similar to a globe artichoke. Actually, they are native to North America where native Americans, who called them sun roots, cultivated and valued them long before Europeans arrived and before they were introduced to Europe early in the seventeenth century.

These knobbly tubers measure up to 4 inches in length and 2 inches in width. The brown-purple skin is thin and hides the crisp and sweet white flesh inside, giving a distinctive flavor to this neglected delicacy. Once your crop is established—it is a hardy perennial—it will continue to produce, growing like a weed, with plenty for the freezer.

However, there is a downside to eating this lovely and rare-flavored vegetable. They have a tendency to cause wind in many people, thus limiting their popularity.

To prepare, scrub and thinly peel under cold running water. Alternatively, they can be boiled in their skins and then peeled. Place in acidulated water (water to which lemon juice or vinegar has been added) to help preserve the color.

They can be roasted like potatoes. Or mashed. To boil, place in water and cook for 25-30 minutes. Jerusalem artichokes are also good steamed or sautéed. They brown beautifully in the pan because of the high sugar content. They can be served with Hollandaise or cheese sauce. And raw slices can enhance vegetable or fruit salads.

RECIPES for JERUSALEM ARTICHOKES

SOUPS

ACCOMPANIMENTS

Jerusalem Artichoke Soup

This winter vegetable is knobbly and fussy to peel, but worth the effort. Its subtle flavor makes a most delicious soup, which also freezes well.

2 oz (50 g) butter
1 large onion, chopped
1 lb (450 g) Jerusalem artichokes, peeled and roughly
  chopped
40 fl oz (1.2 litres or 5 cups) chicken stock
salt and freshly ground black pepper
6 tablespoons light cream
parsley or chives, finely chopped

1. Melt the butter in a saucepan and cook the onion in it over gentle heat, stirring occasionally until the onion is soft.
2. Add the chopped artichokes and cook for a minute or two. Pour on the stock, and bring to the boil. Then simmer gently, covered, for 30 minutes.
3. Remove from heat, and purée in a blender or food processor. Season with salt and pepper.
4. Reheat when ready to serve. Ladle into soup dishes, and add a spoonful of cream to each plateful. Sprinkle some finely chopped parsley or chives on top of each.

Serves 6

Tomato-Jerusalem Artichoke Soup

What an excellent soup this knobby tuber—the Jerusalem artichoke—makes!

1 large onion, chopped
2 tablespoons vegetable or olive oil
1-2 garlic cloves, chopped
3 medium tomatoes
1 lb (450 g) Jerusalem artichokes
40 fl oz (1.2 litres or 5 cups) chicken stock
salt and freshly ground pepper
juice of half a lemon

1. In a large saucepan, sauté the onion in oil until soft. Add the garlic and continue frying for a minute or two.
2. Peel and chop the tomatoes and add to pan. Cook for 5 minutes, stirring frequently.
3. Add the peeled Jerusalem artichokes and the stock. Season with salt and freshly ground pepper. Simmer for about 30-40 minutes, until Jerusalem artichokes are soft.
4. Mash the artichokes (or use a food processor). Reheat if necessary. Add the lemon juice and serve.

Serves 4-6

Chilled Cream of Jerusalem Artichoke Soup

This chilled cream soup freezes well before adding cream.

1½ lbs (700 g) Jerusalem artichokes
juice of half a lemon
2 oz (50 g) butter
1 onion, thinly sliced
¼ cucumber, sliced
30 fl oz (900 ml) chicken stock
10 fl oz (300 ml) dry white wine
6 parsley sprigs
salt and black pepper to taste
5 fl oz (150 ml) double or heavy cream
about 4 oz (100 g) plain yogurt
finely chopped fresh parsley

1. Peel the artichokes and cut them into small chunks. Allow them to stand in a bowl of cold water with the lemon juice (to keep them from turning brown).
2. Melt the butter in a large saucepan and add the sliced onion, sliced cucumber, and drained artichokes to the pan.
3. Cook the vegetables in the butter for 5 minutes over low heat. Do not allow them to brown.
4. Pour in stock and wine. Add the parsley and season with salt and freshly ground pepper. Bring to a boil, then reduce heat and simmer covered for about 20 minutes, or until vegetables are tender. Remove from heat.
5. Purée in a blender or food processor. Chill in refrigerator for at least 3 hours. (Or freeze it at this point.)
6. When ready to serve, blend in the cream. Then ladle the soup into individual bowls, and add a dollop of yogurt on top of each serving. Garnish with chopped fresh parsley.

Serves 8

Jerusalem Artichoke and Carrot Soup

A luscious soup with a creamy texture and an attractive amber color.

1½ lbs (700 g) Jerusalem artichokes
1 lb (450 g) carrots, peeled and sliced
3 oz (75 g) butter
1 medium onion, chopped
3 stalks celery, chopped
50 fl oz (1.5 litres or 6 cups) stock
salt and freshly ground pepper, to taste

1. Peel and slice the artichokes and place them in a bowl of acidulated water.
2. In a large saucepan, gently sauté the onion and celery in the melted butter for 5 minutes. When they are soft, mix in the artichokes and sliced carrots. Cover and simmer for about 10 minutes over low heat.
3. Stir in the stock and mix it all together. Simmer with lid on until vegetables are soft, about 20 minutes. Add salt and freshly ground black pepper.
4. Purée the mixture in a food processor. Reheat before serving.

Serves 6-8

Boiled Jerusalem Artichokes

For a welcome change of menu, serve this simple Jerusalem artichoke dish in place of boiled potatoes.

1 lb (450 g) Jerusalem artichokes
salt
4-6 tablespoons butter, melted
1 tablespoon finely chopped parsley
lemon juice to taste

1. Scrub and pare the Jerusalem artichokes. Place them in a pot of water to cover and add salt. Bring to a boil, then simmer 25-35 minutes, until tender.
2. Drain the artichokes and add the melted butter and chopped parsley and lemon juice.

Serves 4

Baked Jerusalem Artichokes in Butter

A good way to make this vegetable accompaniment.

1½ lbs (700 g) Jerusalem artichokes
juice of half a lemon
1 teaspoon salt
2 oz (50 g) butter
flour seasoned with pepper

1. Peel the artichokes, cut them into thin slices, and drop them into a bowl of water with the lemon juice to prevent them from turning brown.
2. Drain the artichokes and add them, together with salt, to a pot of boiling water. Cook for 4 minutes, then drain.
3. Coat the artichokes in the seasoned flour and then roll them in the butter which has been melted in a flat baking dish. (Use more butter if necessary.)
4. Place the dish in an oven preheated to 350°F (180°C) and bake for about 40 minutes, until golden.

Serves 6

Mashed Jerusalem Artichokes

This dish offers the option of blending the artichokes together with potatoes or carrots to make a mixed root vegetable purée. It can be prepared in the morning and simply reheated for dinner that night. Use whatever quantities you desire.

Jerusalem artichokes
butter
milk
1-2 egg yolks
salt and pepper to taste
potatoes or carrots (optional)

1. Boil Jerusalem artichokes, drain, and mash until smooth. If you are adding potatoes or carrots, cook them together and mash until smooth.
2. Beat with some butter until you have a smooth purée. Add a little bit of milk and 1 or 2 egg yolks, depending on quantity. Season with salt and freshly ground black pepper.
3. Turn into a well-buttered casserole and heat in a medium oven before serving.

Jerusalem Artichokes with Fresh Tomato Sauce

*This lightly cooked and simple tomato sauce goes well with
Jerusalem artichokes and is useful also for other cooked
vegetables such as cauliflower, as well as for pasta.*

1½ lbs (700 g) Jerusalem artichokes
½ oz (15 g) butter
4 tablespoons water
salt
1 onion, chopped
1 tablespoon olive oil
1 lb (450 g) tomatoes, skinned and chopped
salt and freshly ground black pepper to taste

1. Peel Jerusalem artichokes and cut into evenly sized pieces. Place them in a saucepan with butter, water and salt. Cover and cook gently for about 20 minutes or until tender.
2. Meanwhile prepare the tomato sauce by frying the onion in oil for 10 minutes until soft but not brown. Add the tomatoes and cook for an additional 10 minutes, until they are soft. Purée the tomato mixture in a blender or food processor and season with salt and pepper.
3. When Jerusalem artichokes are tender, drain them. Pour the tomato sauce over them and serve.

Serves 6

Jerusalem Artichoke Casserole

A beautiful looking presentation with a taste to match.

1 lb (450 g) Jerusalem artichokes
10 fl oz (½ pint or 300 ml) milk
salt and freshly ground black pepper
pinch grated nutmeg
1 clove garlic, minced
10 fl oz (½ pint or 300 ml) double or heavy cream
2 oz (50 g) cheddar cheese, finely grated

1. Peel artichokes and cut into slices about ¼ inch (.6 cm) thick. Place in acidulated water.
2. Pour milk into a saucepan and add salt and pepper, nutmeg, and minced garlic. Bring to a boil, then add artichoke slices and simmer slowly for about 10 minutes.
3. Drain the artichoke slices. (Reserve milk for some other use as in a soup or sauce.) Spoon artichoke slices into a buttered casserole.
4. Mix the cream with the cheese and bring to a boil in a saucepan. Then pour the cream and cheese mixture over the artichokes.
5. Bake in a preheated oven at 350°F (180°C) until crisp, about 10 minutes.

Serves 6

Leeks

LEEKS

Leeks have a long history. They were grown in ancient Egypt and continued to be eaten throughout the Greek and Roman periods. In more recent times, in the seventeenth and eighteenth centuries, they were more popular with rural communities and came to be dubbed "poor man's asparagus" because they grow easily in so many climates and make reasonable meals for struggling families

The easiest of the onion family to grow, leeks commonly find their way into soups and stews. With a sweet taste that is less pungent than onion, they are valuable for adding flavor but may also be cooked on their own as a vegetable. They may be braised and eaten hot or cold—a favorite first course in France. Or, sliced and gently sautéed in butter, they make an excellent filling for an omelet or quiche. They are done cooking when easily pierced with a thin-bladed knife.

Leeks do not even need to be cooked. Sliced and mixed with shredded cabbage, and tossed with dressing, they make a good winter salad.

Allow enough time for careful washing. After cutting off the root end and tough leaf ends and removing tough outer leaves, cut the leeks in half lengthwise leaving root end intact and wash well under cold running water to remove any dirt or grit lodged between the layers. Leeks can also be left whole or sliced into rings.

Leeks can be kept for months when they are loosely wrapped in plastic and stored in the refrigerator.

RECIPES for LEEKS

SOUPS

APPETIZERS

ACCOMPANIMENTS

Leek and Potato Soup

The flavor of this warm and filling soup, not very high in calories, may be heightened with the addition of a little bit of curry powder.

2 oz (50 g) butter
1 large onion, chopped
6 large leeks, washed and cut into 1 inch (2.5 cm) long pieces
1 stalk celery, chopped (optional)
3 medium potatoes, peeled and chopped
2-3 teaspoons curry powder (optional)
36 fl oz (1 litre or 4 ½ cups) chicken stock
salt and freshly ground black pepper

1. Melt the butter in a saucepan, add the chopped onion and cook gently, stirring occasionally, for about 10 minutes, or until the onion is transparent.
2. Add the leeks, celery, and potatoes and cook for another 5 minutes, stirring occasionally.
3. Stir in the curry powder and cook for another minute or two. Add the stock and bring contents to the boil, then simmer gently for 30-45 minutes, until the potato is cooked.
4. Remove the saucepan from the heat, cool and purée in a blender or food processor. Season to taste.
5. Reheat when ready to serve.

Serves 6-8

Vichyssoise

This is a delicious and elegant cold soup to serve on a summer evening; it relies on cream, unlike its hot potato and leek counterpart.

4 leeks, white part, sliced
1 medium onion, sliced
2 oz (50 g) butter
5 medium potatoes, thinly sliced
32 fl oz (900 ml or 4 cups) chicken stock
1-2 teaspoons salt, or to taste
freshly ground black pepper
24 fl oz (700 ml or 3 cups) milk
16 fl oz (450 ml or 2 cups) heavy cream
chopped chives

1. Melt the butter in a large saucepan. Add the well-washed and sliced leeks and the sliced onion. Lightly cook until soft, about 15 minutes.
2. Add the potatoes, stock and seasonings. Cook for 30 minutes or until very tender. Purée in a blender or food processor.
3. Return the processed mixture to the saucepan. Add the milk and half the cream and bring to a boil. Sieve and chill.
4. Add the remaining cream and chill thoroughly.
5. Serve very cold, sprinkling with a garnish of chives before serving.

Serves 8

Cock-A-Leekie Soup

This traditional Scottish soup is said to have originated from cockfighting days when the loser was thrown into the soup. The prunes add extra flavor.

1 chicken, about 3 lbs or 1.4 kg
1 tablespoon salt
6 peppercorns
6 leeks
6 prunes
chopped parsley

1. Place chicken in a large pot with enough cold water to cover it. Add salt and peppercorns (placed in a metal tea strainer or wrapped in cheese cloth for easy removal later on) and bring to a boil. Skim off any scum that may be on top. Cover and simmer for about 1½ hours.
2. Trim the leeks to within 2 inches (5 cm) of the white stems. Then split the leeks lengthways, wash them well, and cut them into 1 inch (2.5 cm) pieces.
3. Skim the soup again, add the leeks and prunes, and simmer for another 30 minutes.
4. Take the chicken out of the pot and remove the skin and bones from it. Keep the breast pieces for another recipe. Cut the remaining meat into small pieces and add to the soup. Remove peppercorns and correct seasonings.
5. Sprinkle finely chopped parsley over the hot soup just before serving.

Serves 6

Leek Brotchan

Brotchan, an Irish word for broth, is usually made from leeks and potatoes or other vegetables. The butter beans used in this recipe give the soup a delicate color and a creamy texture.

5 oz (150 g) butter beans
35 fl oz (1 litre) water for soaking
35 fl oz (1 litre) water for cooking
3 leeks, washed and sliced
2 oz (50 g) butter
35 fl oz (1 litre) stock
2 oz (50 g) parsley, chopped
juice of half a lemon
1 tablespoon white wine vinegar
salt and pepper
cream to garnish

1. Soak the beans in water overnight.
2. Drain and rinse them. Place the beans in a saucepan of fresh water and boil for 10 minutes. Then simmer in partially covered saucepan for an additional 40-45 minutes, until the beans are soft. Drain.
3. Melt butter in a saucepan and cook the sliced leeks gently for 4-5 minutes. Then add the beans and cook for an additional 5 minutes, stirring occasionally. Add the stock and simmer, covered, for 20 minutes. Stir in the chopped parsley and allow soup to cool slightly.
4. Purée using a food processor and return to pot. Reheat, adding lemon juice and vinegar to taste, and season with salt and freshly ground black pepper.
5. Spoon the hot soup into bowls and garnish each serving with a spoonful of cream.

Serves 6-8

Leek Paté

This is a vegetarian starter that is certain to please your guests and become a favorite.

2 lbs (1 kg) leeks
1 potato about 9 oz (250 g)
3 eggs, lightly beaten
2½ oz (60 g) grated Parmesan cheese
¼ teaspoon nutmeg
pepper
3 tablespoons sunflower oil

1. Wash leeks thoroughly under cold running water and remove the coarse outer leaves and green ends. Then boil the leeks until they are very soft. Drain, pressing out as much water as you can.
2. Boil and drain the potato.
3. In a food processor, purée the leeks. Add the potato, cut into pieces. Add the remaining ingredients, setting aside 1-2 tablespoons grated cheese and 1 tablespoon oil for the topping. Blend.
4. Transfer the mixture to a greased baking dish. Sprinkle the reserved cheese and oil over the top.
5. Bake in an oven preheated to 400°F (200°C) for 35-40 minutes, until it is firm and has a lightly browned top.

Serves 6

Leek Tart

*With leek season from August to May, think of making this
delicious tart when the first young leeks appear at the end of
August. It can be used as a main course to serve four people or
as an appetizer to serve six.*

4 tablespoons butter
6 leeks, thinly sliced
2 eggs plus 2 egg yolks
8 fl oz (225 ml or 1 cup) light or single cream
8 fl oz (225 ml or 1 cup) heavy or double cream
salt and freshly ground black pepper
ground nutmeg (optional)
1 partially baked 9-inch (22.8 cm) pie shell
2-3 oz (50-75 g) grated Gruyère cheese

1. Melt the butter in a frying pan. Add the sliced leeks and cook,
   covered, over low heat until they are tender, about 30 minutes.
   Stir frequently to prevent them from browning. Remove from
   heat.
2. In a bowl, whisk together the eggs, egg yolks, light and heavy
   cream. Season with salt and freshly ground black pepper. Add
   a pinch of nutmeg if you want to.
3. Turn the cooled leek mixture into a partially baked tart shell.
   Add the egg and cream mixture, filling the shell to within ½
   inch (1.2 cm) of the top. Sprinkle Gruyère over the top.
4. Bake on middle shelf of an oven preheated to 300°F (150°C)
   for 35-45 minutes, until the top is browned and filling is set.
5. Allow to cool for 10 minutes before cutting into wedges.
   Serve warm.

Serves 4-6

Leeks à la Grecque

A lovely and refreshing first course for a summer meal.

16 fl oz (450 ml or 2 cups) water
4 fl oz (100 ml or ½ cup) olive oil
juice of 1 large lemon
½ teaspoon salt
12 black peppercorns
12 fennel seeds or 1 branch fennel
6 coriander seeds
1 stalk celery, cut up
6 sprigs parsley
1-2 shallots, finely chopped
1 lb (450 g) leeks
finely chopped fresh herbs to garnish

1. In a large pot, combine all ingredients except the leeks and garnishing herbs. Bring to a boil, then simmer for 10 minutes, stirring occasionally.
2. Add the well-cleaned, sliced leeks and simmer for another 15 minutes.
3. Remove the leeks to a serving dish. Reduce the cooking liquid by boiling rapidly. Strain the liquid over the leeks and chill.
4. Sprinkle with chopped fresh herbs and serve.

Serves 4-6

Leeks Nicoise

French vegetable dishes prepared à la Nicoise suggest the inclusion of tomatoes and garlic. This dish can be served cold as a starter—it's great for al fresco dining—or hot with grilled fish, meat or chicken.

12 leeks
3-4 tablespoons olive oil
3 tomatoes, skinned and roughly chopped
2 large cloves garlic, finely minced
4 oz (100 g or ½ cup) black or Nicoise olives
1 tablespoon fresh chopped parsley
2 tablespoons lemon juice
freshly ground pepper

1. Cut off the roots and trim the green tops, cutting them to make the leeks even in length. Rinse thoroughly, then pat dry using paper towels.
2. Heat the oil in a large frying pan over medium heat and arrange the leeks in it. Fry until they are lightly colored underneath, then turn over. Sprinkle with pepper, cover, and continue to cook over low heat for about 12 minutes or longer, until the white part is tender. Remove leeks and set them aside.
3. Add the tomatoes, crushed garlic, olives, and parsley to the frying pan and cook for 2-3 minutes, stirring frequently. Adjust seasoning and add lemon juice. Return leeks to the pan to heat if necessary.
4. Place leeks on a serving platter, pouring contents of the frying pan over them and serve. Or refrigerate and serve cold when ready.

Serves 6

Leeks Vinaigrette

*This easy recipe makes a fine winter salad that can accompany a
main course or make a good first course.*

12 medium leeks
4 tablespoons French dressing
1 garlic clove, minced (optional)
1 tablespoon finely chopped parsley

1. Wash and trim leeks. Leave them whole or cut them in half
   lengthways. Simmer them in salted water for about 10-12
   minutes, until they are just tender. Drain well and arrange
   them in a shallow serving dish.
2. While they are still warm, coat each leek with French dressing.
   (Mix a minced garlic clove into the dressing, if you want to.)
3. Sprinkle with chopped parsley and refrigerate until ready to
   serve.

Serves 4-6

Leek and Carrot Salad

Another appealing first course. Serve with warm brown rolls.

6 leeks, washed and cut into slices about 3/8 inch (1cm) long
2 oz (50 g) butter
2 onions, finely cut into slivers
2 rounded teaspoons ground ginger
4 medium carrots, peeled and grated
4 tomatoes, skinned, seeded and puréed in a blender
5 oz (150 g) yogurt
1 rounded tablespoon chopped parsley
salt and freshly ground black pepper
more parsley to garnish

1. In a frying pan, melt the butter and add the sliced leeks. Cook over low heat, stirring occasionally, until the leeks are soft, about 10-15 minutes. Remove them from the pan and place them in a shallow serving dish.
2. Cook the sliced onions in the frying pan over low heat until they are soft and transparent. Sprinkle in the ground ginger and mix well together with the onions. Remove the onions from the pan and arrange them evenly over the leeks.
3. Place grated carrots in a bowl. Mix together the puréed tomato, yogurt, parsley, and salt and pepper, and pour this mixture over the carrots. Blend it all together well.
4. Put the carrot mixture over the onions and leeks. Sprinkle top with a little chopped parsley.

Serves 6-8

Lemon Leeks

This easy method of preparing a good side dish of leeks can be varied by the addition of tarragon.

6 leeks
1 teaspoon minced fresh tarragon leaves or ½ teaspoon dried tarragon (optional)
2 tablespoons butter
2 tablespoons fresh lemon juice

1. Strip away the coarse outer leaves, cut off most of the green tops, and wash very carefully between the layers to remove all traces of grit. Cut into ¾ inch (2 cm) lengths.
2. Steam the leeks until tender, about 10-15 minutes, adding tarragon if you want to. Transfer to a serving dish.
3. Melt the butter and add lemon juice. Pour the mixture over the cooked leeks.

Serves 4

Grilled Leeks

While this is especially appetizing prepared on the outdoor barbecue, these leeks can also be done indoors using a conventional grill.

about 2 lbs (1 kg) leeks
olive oil
salt and pepper

1. Brush the cleaned and trimmed leeks lightly with olive oil. Sprinkle with salt and freshly ground black pepper. If leeks are thin, place them in a grilling basket before putting them on the grill (so that they can be turned over all at once).
2. Turn the leeks occasionally while grilling until they are tender and nicely browned, 10-15 minutes, depending on thickness.
3. Serve with vinaigrette or any flavored oil such as chili oil.

Serves 4-6

Fried Leeks

This dish, which goes well with grilled or roast meat, will also help to use up your crop of tomatoes.

2 lbs (1 kg) leeks
6 tablespoons olive oil
2 cloves garlic
1 bay leaf
salt and black pepper
4 tomatoes, peeled and chopped
juice of half a lemon

1. Strip away the coarse outer green leaves and cut off the green tips of the leeks. Slice them in half lengthwise. Wash under cold running water to remove all the dirt, and cut into 1 inch (2.5 cm) slices.
2. Heat 3 tablespoons of the oil in a large frying pan and add the leeks. Crush the garlic over them. Add the bay leaf and the salt and freshly ground black pepper to taste.
3. Cover and cook over low heat for 20 minutes.
4. Skin the tomatoes by immersing them in hot or boiled water for 1 minute. Chop.
5. Add the chopped tomatoes and the remaining 3 tablespoons of the oil to the pan. Cook for another 5 minutes. Remove the bay leaf and transfer the leeks to a serving dish. Drizzle with the lemon juice and serve.

Serves 4-6

Fried Leeks and Rice

The leek and rice combination makes a superb side dish that complements meat courses.

2 lbs (900 g) leeks
6 oz (175 g) rice
1 tablespoon salt
2 oz (50 g) butter
½ teaspoon curry powder
freshly ground black pepper

1. Trim the leeks and wash them well under cold running water to remove any grit that is lodged between the leaves. Cut into slices ¼ inch (.6 cm) thick.
2. Cook the rice in a large pot of boiling salted water, covered, for about 15 minutes.
3. Meanwhile, place leeks in a pot of boiling water and simmer for about 5 minutes. Drain them in a colander.
4. Melt the butter in a frying pan and sauté the leeks until tender, about 5 minutes.
5. Add the cooked and drained rice to the leeks in the frying pan. Blend in the curry powder and fry for a few minutes longer, stirring continuously. Season with pepper and serve.

Serves 8

Ottoman-Style Leeks

*With a hint of exotic Middle Eastern cuisine, this intriguing
vegetarian side dish can also be served as a starter, perhaps
with hot nan bread.*

**4 good-sized leeks
1 onion, chopped
4 tablespoons olive oil
2 handfuls of mint
2 handfuls of flat-leaf parsley
2 tablespoons pine kernels
salt and pepper
can of chickpeas
Greek style yogurt**

1. Trim the leeks and slice the white and pale green parts into rings about ½ inch (1.2 cm) thick. Wash thoroughly and allow them to dry in a colander.
2. Sauté chopped onion in olive oil until tender and golden.
3. Stir leeks into the onion. Add a handful of chopped mint and a handful of chopped parsley. Add more oil if needed. Stir in pine kernels. Season with salt and pepper.
4. Cook covered, stirring from time to time for about 15 minutes, until leeks are tender.
5. Drain the chickpeas and rinse under cold running water. Mix them into the pan and heat through. Adjust seasonings.
6. Just before serving, stir in another handful of chopped mint and a handful of parsley.
7. Serve hot or cold, garnished with a spoonful of yogurt.

Serves 4-6

Leeks and Kohlrabi

Kohlrabi, with a mild flavor that is reminiscent of water chestnuts, is a vegetable that is recently becoming more popular. Whether you grow your own, or have some other vested interest, it's worth sampling this simple way of mixing it with leeks.

4 medium leeks
8 kohlrabi, 1½-2 inches (3.8-5 cm) in diameter
4 tablespoons butter
salt and pepper to taste

1. Trim the roots and dark green leaves from the leeks. Split them lengthwise and wash thoroughly. Cut crosswise into very thin slices, about 1/8 inch (.3 cm).
2. Peel the kohlrabi and cut into thin slices.
3. In a large frying pan, melt the butter and add the kohlrabi. Sauté for 2 to 3 minutes.
4. Add the leeks and continue to sauté until vegetables have begun to soften. Season and serve.

Serves 4-6

Leeks in Mornay Sauce

Mornay is a cheese sauce that offers another great recipe to add to your leek repertory.

8-10 medium leeks
16 fl oz (450 ml or 2 cups) chicken stock
3 fl oz (75 ml) dry white wine
3 tablespoons butter
2 oz (50 g or ¼ cup) flour
2 tablespoons heavy or double cream
salt and pepper
8 oz (225 g) shredded Gruyère or other Swiss cheese

1. Wash leeks thoroughly. Cut white part into 1-inch (2.5 cm) lengths.
2. Place stock and wine in a saucepan and bring to a boil. Add the leeks and lower heat. Cover saucepan and simmer for about 10 to 12 minutes, or until leeks are tender.
3. With a slotted spoon, transfer leeks to a casserole, reserving the liquid.
4. Melt butter in a saucepan over medium heat. Blend in the flour and cook for a minute or two. Stir in the reserved stock and wine mixture. Add the cream. Cook and stir until the mixture thickens and comes to a boil.
5. Add three quarters of the Swiss cheese and continue stirring until cheese is melted. Remove from heat and pour over leeks.
6. Sprinkle remaining cheese over the top. Before serving, place casserole under broiler until the cheese browns and sauce is bubbly.

Serves 6

Onions and Shallots

ONIONS and SHALLOTS

The varieties of onion are many—ranging in color and strength and size. Among the varieties are Spanish onions, yellow onions, white onions, Vidalia onions, and spring onions or scallions. Even the same variety of onion can change as the season progresses.

Shallots, members of the onion family, are small and slender with long necks and golden skins. Their flavor is delicate and less intense than most onions and should be used whenever specified in recipes, or when a fine flavor is called for, especially in sauces.

Onion sets are immature bulbs for planting that have a few advantages over seed: they are more successful, quick maturing, and not prone to onion fly or mildew attack.

This versatile vegetable is supposed to aid digestion, cure colds, and enable sleep. Among the methods that abound for peeling onions without tears is to peel under running cold tap water.

As an addition to flavor dishes—in soups, stews, casseroles, sauces—the onion is the most used of all vegetables. It is a kitchen staple that can be used cooked or raw, in prepared dishes, or on its own. On its own as a hot vegetable, it can be boiled, baked, stir-fried, or glazed. Onion rings are another popular use.

Culinary uses are so varied that the recipes selected here are ones that make full use of this basic vegetable.

RECIPES for ONIONS AND SHALLOTS

SOUPS
Onion Soup   120
Creamy Onion Soup   121
Onion Tomato Soup   122
Spanish Onion and Potato Soup   123

CONDIMENTS AND SAUCES
Onion Relish   124
Onion Salsa   125
Pickled Onions   126

APPETIZERS AND SALADS
Onion Appetizers   127
Onion À La Grecque   128
French Onion Tart   129
Onion Salad   130
Onion and Orange Salad   131

ACCOMPANIMENTS
Barbecued Spanish Onions   132
Roasted Spanish Onions   133
Onions with Cream and Sherry   134
Onions with Apples   135
Glazed Small Onions or Shallots   136
Caramelized Onions   137
Onion Gratin Casserole   138
Onion Squares   139
Fried Onion Rings   140

MAIN DISHES
Spanish Onion Omelette   141
Caramelized Onions with Lentils and Rice   142
Stuffed Onions   144

Onion Soup

A rich and full bodied beef stock is the main ingredient of this soup which gives the most wonderful onion aroma while it is cooking. To make it in the French style, spoon the soup into individual ovenproof bowls and top with croûtes or French bread rounds sprinkled with grated Parmesan cheese and shredded Gruyère. Bake at 400°F (200°C) until cheese melts. Place bowls under broiler to brown the cheese.

3 lbs (1.4 kg) onions (yellow), peeled and thinly sliced
3 tablespoons butter
2 tablespoons oil
1 teaspoon sugar
48 fl oz (1.5 litres or 6 cups) beef broth
1 teaspoon Worcestershire sauce
1 clove garlic, minced
1 bay leaf
salt and freshly ground black pepper
2 fl oz (50 ml or ¼ cup) dry sherry
grated Parmesan cheese

1. Peel onions and slice them thinly.
2. Heat the butter and oil in a large pot. Stir in the sliced onions and sprinkle sugar over them. Cook over medium heat, stirring occasionally, for about 15-20 minutes or until onions are soft and transparent. Raise the heat and cook for another 20 minutes, stirring frequently, until onions become gold or pale brown. Be careful not to burn the onions.
3. Add the broth, Worcestershire sauce, garlic, bay leaf, salt and pepper.
4. Cover, raise heat, and bring to a boil. Then, lower heat and simmer for 20 minutes. Remove the bay leaf and stir in the sherry. Sprinkle with cheese and serve.

Serves 6-8

Creamy Onion Soup

This rich soup contains a variety of onions ranging from ordinary yellow ones to a garnish of chives, the mildest member of the onion family.

4 tablespoons butter
2 medium-large yellow onions, finely chopped
4 large leeks, white parts only, thinly sliced
2-3 shallots, chopped
4-6 garlic cloves, minced
32 fl oz (1 litre or 4 cups) chicken stock
1 teaspoon dried thyme
1 bay leaf
salt and pepper to taste
8 fl oz (250 ml or 1 cup) double or heavy cream
3 spring onions (scallions), sliced into ½ inch (1.2 cm) lengths
toasted French bread croutons
fresh chives, cut up, for garnish

1. Melt the butter in a large saucepan. Add the onions, leeks, shallots and garlic. Cook over low heat with the lid on for about 20-25 minutes. Vegetables should be tender and golden.
2. Pour in stock, and add thyme, bay leaf, salt and freshly ground pepper. Bring to a boil, then reduce heat, and simmer for 20 minutes, with lid partly covering.
3. Strain the soup into a bowl. Transfer the solids together with 1 cup of the liquid to a food processor and purée the mixture.
4. Combine the purée and the remaining liquid in the saucepan and place over medium heat. Whisk in the cream, bringing the mixture to a simmer. Add the spring onions and simmer for 5 minutes.
5. Serve in hot bowls, garnished with French bread croutons and fresh chives.

Serves 4-6

Onion Tomato Soup

A variation on friendly and flavorful onion soup.

2 large onions, chopped
3 tablespoons olive or vegetable oil
3 oz (80 g or ½ cup) fine noodles, crushed
6 oz (170 g) tomato paste or purée
32 fl oz (900 ml or 4 cups) water
2 teaspoons powdered chicken soup mix
½ teaspoon salt
¼ teaspoon pepper or to taste

1. In a large saucepan, sauté onions in the oil over medium heat until they are lightly browned.
2. Crush the noodles with your hands and add them to the onions. Continue cooking, stirring frequently, until noodles are light brown.
3. Add remaining ingredients. Bring to a boil, then simmer with cover on for 15 minutes.

Serves 4-6

Spanish Onion and Potato Soup

An appetizing and hearty cold-weather soup to be served with crusty bread.

4 medium onions
2 tablespoons olive oil
32 fl oz (1 litre or 4 cups) water
2-3 medium potatoes
2 teaspoons paprika
1 teaspoon fresh thyme (½ teaspoon dried)
2 bay leaves
2 fl oz (50 ml or ¼ cup) dry sherry
salt and freshly ground black pepper to taste
pinch of saffron
dash of hot pepper sauce or pinch of cayenne (optional)
fresh parsley, chopped

1. Cut the onions in half and slice them thinly. In a large pot, sauté the onions in the oil, stirring from time to time to keep them from sticking. Meanwhile, boil the water in a separate pan.
2. When onions are transparent, add the paprika, thyme, and bay leaves. Sauté for 1 minute. Pour the boiling water into the onion mixture.
3. Cut the potatoes lengthwise into quarters, then slice into small wedge-shaped pieces ¼ inch (.6 cm) thick and add them to the pot. Add sherry, salt, and pepper. Return to a boil, cover pot and simmer for about 10 minutes. Add the saffron and continue cooking until the potatoes are tender.
4. Remove bay leaves. Add hot pepper sauce or cayenne, if you want to.
5. Ladle the soup into bowls and garnish with chopped parsley.

Serves 4-6

Onion Relish

This piquant relish offers variety and a superb flavor contrast when served with a savory dish.

24 small white onions
3 fl oz (75 ml or 1/3 cup) olive oil
3 fl oz (75 ml or 1/3 cup) white wine vinegar
10 fl oz (300 ml or 1¼ cups) water
1-2 cloves garlic, chopped
½ teaspoon salt
½ teaspoon dry mustard
½ teaspoon mustard seed
½ teaspoon freshly ground black pepper
1 clove
1 teaspoon sugar
2-3 oz (50-75 g) light raisins
minced parsley or dill

1. Boil the unpeeled onions for 5 minutes. Drain and remove the skins.
2. Combine the oil, vinegar, water, seasonings, and sugar in a large pan. Add onions and simmer until onions are just tender, about 15 minutes. Add raisins and simmer a further three minutes. Cool.
3. Sprinkle the chilled relish with parsley or dill and serve.

Serves 6

Onion Salsa

*Inspired by such South-of-the-border Mexican dishes as
quesadillas or enchiladas, this sauce can also add zest to any
ordinary grilled or roasted meat course. The number of chilies
you add will determine how hot this sauce is.*

**1 large onion, coarsely chopped
1-2 fresh chilies (or more if desired), stemmed and seeded
2 garlic cloves, minced
3 fl oz (75 ml) fresh lemon or lime juice
4 tablespoons fresh chopped cilantro or parsley
small fresh tomato, chopped
1 tablespoon olive oil
salt to taste**

1. Blend all ingredients together in a food processor or blender
   until smooth. This sauce keeps well in refrigerator for 3 to 4
   days.

Pickled Onions

Here is an obvious way to deal with a bumper crop of onions.

3 lbs (1.5 kg) small white onions
4 oz (100 g or ½ cup) salt
1-2 red chili peppers, or more, seeded and quartered
½ teaspoon peppercorns
4 pieces ginger root
2-8 oz (50-225g) sugar (according to taste)
48 fl oz (1.3 litres or 6 cups) white vinegar

1. Put even-sized onions, unpeeled, in boiling water to cover and allow to stand for two minutes. Drain. Cover them with cold water and peel.
2. Using a large steel or pottery container, dissolve the salt in 4 cups (32 fl oz or 900 ml) of water. Add the onions and more water to cover, if needed. Allow to stand overnight. Rinse in cold water and drain.
3. Bring to a boil enough water to cover the onions. Immerse the onions and cook them for 1 minute. Drain.
4. Layer the onions in hot clean jars with pepper, peppercorns, and ginger root.
5. Combine the sugar and vinegar and bring to a boil. Pour the mixture over the onions up to ½ inch (1.2 cm) from the top of the jar. Seal.
6. Allow to stand for 2-3 months before using.

Onion Appetizers

To insure success of this fine appetizer, use good quality bread and wafer-thin onion slices.

any fine-textured bread such as brioche or challah
small onions, cut into very thin slices
mayonnaise
salt
finely chopped parsley

1. Cut the bread into slices about ¼ inch (.6 cm) thick. Using a biscuit cutter, or the open end of a sherry or whiskey glass, cut out rounds from the slices about 1¼ inches (3 cm) in diameter.
2. Slice small raw onions to nearly transparent thinness, making each round just a little smaller than the bread rounds.
3. Spread mayonnaise on bread rounds. Arrange an onion slice on half the pieces and sprinkle with salt. Cover the onion with the remaining bread rounds to form a sandwich.
4. Spread mayonnaise on a board, and sprinkle chopped parsley on another board. Hold each sandwich gently between thumb and forefinger and turn it like a wheel, rolling the edge first in mayonnaise, then in parsley.
5. Place completed sandwiches on a flat tray. Chill thoroughly before serving.

Onions à la Grecque

This top-notch first course, which should be served cold, makes an especially refreshing starter for a summer meal. Or you can make it part of mixed hors d'oeuvres.

1½ lbs (700 g) small or baby onions
10 fl oz (300 ml) water
20 fl oz (600 ml) dry white wine
5 tablespoons olive oil
juice of 1 large lemon
12 black peppercorns
12 fennel seeds
6 coriander seeds
6 sprigs parsley
1-2 shallots, chopped
1 bay leaf
½ teaspoon salt
finely chopped parsley to garnish

1. Peel onions and set aside.
2. Prepare an aromatic sauce by combining the remaining ingredients except garnish in a large saucepan. Bring to a boil, then simmer for 10 minutes. Add the prepared onions and continue to simmer for 10-15 minutes or until they are tender.
3. Transfer onions to a serving dish.
4. Boil cooking liquid to reduce it by half. Strain through a sieve over the onions.
5. Chill in refrigerator for at least several hours. To serve, spoon onions with sauce into soup plates and garnish with parsley.

Serves 6

French Onion Tart

Alsace is the source for this rich creamy flan that can be served hot or cold, as a main course with a green salad, or cut into wedges for a first course.

1 9-inch (22.8 cm) pastry-lined flan dish
1 lb (450 g) onions, thinly sliced
2 oz (50 g) butter
1 bay leaf
salt and pepper
2 eggs
grated nutmeg
5 fl oz (150 ml) double or heavy cream
5 fl oz (150 ml) milk

1. Prepare pastry: sift 4 oz flour with a pinch of salt and rub in 3 oz (75 g) butter. Beat an egg yolk with a teaspoon cold water and mix it all together. It should come away cleanly from the bowl. Roll it out on a floured board and line the flan dish. Trim the edge and prick the base with a fork.
2. Melt butter in a frying pan and add the sliced onions and bay leaf. Sprinkle with salt and pepper to taste. Cover the pan with a lid and cook over low heat for about 20 minutes, until the onions are quite soft and golden. Stir occasionally to prevent sticking. Remove bay leaf when done.
3. In a large bowl, lightly beat the eggs and season with salt, pepper and nutmeg. Beat in the cream and milk. Mix thoroughly into the onions and turn into the pastry case.
4. Bake in a hot oven preheated to 400°F (200°C) for 35-40 minutes, until the pastry is golden and the filling is set.

Serves 4-6

Onion Salad

This dish from France, to prepare in advance, will your meal enhance.

4 medium onions
3 tablespoons olive oil
1 tablespoon lemon juice
chopped parsley
capers (optional)

1. Place onions in a roasting pan lined with aluminum foil (to avoid sticking to pan) in an oven preheated to 350°F (180°C).
2. Bake for 1-1½ hours, until they feel soft when tested with a skewer.
3. Peel off the outer skins and cut the onions into quarters. Place on a serving dish.
2. Mix olive oil and lemon juice and drizzle this dressing over the onions. Prepare additional dressing, in proportion, if you use more onions.
3. Garnish with chopped parsley and a few capers, if desired. Serve cold.

Serves 4

Onion and Orange Salad

Delicious, attractive, and easy to prepare, this slightly exotic salad is an excellent accompaniment to Mediterranean menus.

6 large oranges
3 tablespoons red wine vinegar or raspberry vinegar
6 tablespoons olive oil
1 teaspoon oregano
1 medium onion, peeled and very thinly sliced
about 4 oz (110 g or 1 cup) black olives
freshly ground black pepper
fresh chives for garnish

1. Slice the peeled oranges into 4 or 5 crosswise rounds and place them in a shallow serving dish.
2. Drizzle vinegar and olive oil over them and sprinkle with oregano. Toss gently and chill in refrigerator for at least 30 minutes.
3. Remove from refrigerator and toss again. Then arrange the onion slices and olives over the top. Sprinkle with freshly ground black pepper and garnish with chives.

Serves 6-8

Barbecued Spanish Onions

This simple method, which can use any large onion, is ideal for the outdoor barbecue. Peeling in advance is not necessary as the skin can be easily removed after it is cooked.

4 medium-large onions
olive oil
salt and pepper to taste

1. Cut the ends from each onion to allow it to sit flat on the grill. Cut each onion in half across its diameter.
2. Brush both halves with olive oil and sprinkle with salt and freshly ground black pepper.
3. Grill for about 15 minutes, turning occasionally until both sides are tender and browned.

Serves 4

Roasted Spanish Onions

Roasting onions whole brings out the sweet flavor, especially of large Spanish onions, which are milder and easier to handle than other types. With a variety of optional toppings to embellish this tasty accompaniment, you might go through your crop in a short time.

6 large Spanish onions
6 teaspoons butter or olive oil
salt and freshly ground black pepper to taste
optional toppings: butter, sour cream, freshly grated
    Parmesan, crumbled blue cheese, mixed fresh herbs

1. Wash the onions but don't bother to peel as the skins come off easily after cooking and also help to retain the shape of the onion. Cut off the roots and stand onions up in a foil-lined roasting pan or baking dish. (The foil will keep the sugar in the onions from sticking to the pan).
2. Open the tops of each onion slightly, making a deep cut with a pointed knife. Place a bit of butter or oil into each. Sprinkle with salt and pepper.
3. Roast in an oven preheated to 375°F (190°C) for an hour or more, until they are quite tender. (Test with a skewer.)
4. Remove pan from the oven. Peel skins off the onions and place them on a hot serving dish. Spread the onions open, garnish with herbs or any of the optional toppings, and serve.

Serves 6

Onions with Cream and Sherry

An appetizing dish of onions to serve with a main course.

12 medium onions, cut into slices
6 fl oz (175 ml or ¾ cup) cream
3 tablespoons sherry
salt to taste
freshly ground black pepper
3 tablespoons butter

1. Boil the sliced onions for about ten minutes or until they are tender but firm. Drain in a colander and transfer them to a greased baking dish.
2. In a small bowl, mix together the cream, sherry, salt, and pepper. Pour the mixture over the onions and place dots of butter over the top.
3. Cover and bake in an oven preheated to 350°F (180°C) for about 30 minutes.

Serves 6

Onions with Apples

A perfect autumn or winter choice to serve with a roast.

3 medium onions, peeled and sliced
2 tablespoons olive oil
3 medium apples, peeled and sliced
pinch of cinnamon
salt and pepper to taste
fresh chopped parsley for garnish (optional)

1. Place the sliced onions in a large, non-stick frying pan over medium heat. Cover pan and cook for 10 minutes, stirring occasionally. Do not allow to burn. Stir in the oil.
2. Mix in the apples and spices. Cover and cook over low heat, stirring from time to time until apples begin to soften, about 10 minutes.
3. Uncover and cook over medium heat for a few more minutes until apples are tender but not soggy.
4. Garnish with parsley if you want to and serve.

Serves 4

Glazed Small Onions or Shallots

Tasty and attractive, these buttered onions complement elaborate courses of meat. Double the recipe for a dinner party.

1 lb (450 kg) button onions or small yellow onions or shallots
2 oz (50 g) butter
2 tablespoons sugar (or less)

1. Use onions that are about 1 inch (2.5 cm) in diameter. Bring a saucepan of water to the boil and add the washed onions. Cook over low heat for 5 to 7 minutes. Drain, then peel the onions.
2. Melt the butter in a saucepan. Put the onions in the pan and gently stir them over low heat for 3-4 minutes. Add the sugar. Continue stirring and cooking for an additional 4 minutes or until the onions are tender and glazed. Turn the contents into a serving dish.

Serves 4

Caramelized Onions

The lemon juice gives this accompaniment a sweet and sour caramelized flavor and makes it a good choice for enlivening bland foods.

1½ lbs (750 g) small pickling onions or shallots
3 tablespoons olive oil
3 tablespoons sugar
juice of 1½ lemons
8 fl oz (250 ml) water

1. Place the unpeeled onions or shallots in boiling water and cook for about 5 minutes to make the skins easier to remove. Drain and peel off the skins.
2. Heat the oil and sugar in a large pan until the sugar turns brown. Add the onions and stir. Add lemon juice and water.
3. Simmer with cover on for 15 minutes. Then remove the lid and simmer uncovered for 15 minutes until the liquid is reduced to a thick and rich sauce.
4. Transfer to a serving dish.

Serves 6

Onion Gratin Casserole

Casseroles are so practical for company dinners because they can be prepared ahead and simply placed in the oven to bake at the necessary time.

3 medium onions (1 lb or 500 kg), peeled and sliced (or small whole white onions)
2 tablespoons butter
2 tablespoons flour
4 fl oz (100 ml or ½ cup) light or single cream
salt and freshly ground black pepper to taste
2 tablespoons chopped parsley
1 teaspoon thyme (optional)
3-4 tablespoons grated Parmesan cheese

1. Boil the onions until they are just tender, about 15-20 minutes. Drain well, setting aside the cooking liquid. Spoon onions into a casserole.
2. In a saucepan, melt the butter. Blend in the flour with a whisk. Bring the milk to a boil and add to the butter and flour mixture, stirring briskly with the whisk. Add 4 fl oz (100 ml or ½ cup) of the reserved cooking liquid. Mix in salt and pepper and parsley. Add thyme if you want to.
3. Add the sauce to the onions in the casserole and stir together. If you are preparing this recipe in advance, stop at this point. Refrigerate casserole and continue when you are ready.
4. Sprinkle with grated cheese.
5. If you have prepared this dish in advance, bake uncovered in an oven preheated to 375°F (190°C) until it is hot throughout and top is brown. Otherwise, simply brown the dish under a preheated grill.

Serves 4

Onion Squares

A savory accompaniment to a main course.

2 medium onions, sliced
3 tablespoons butter
10 oz (275 g or 2 cups) flour
2 teaspoons baking powder
1 teaspoon salt
about 3 oz (100 g) butter or shortening
8 fl oz (225 ml or 1 cup) milk
2 tablespoons chopped parsley
4 oz (110 g or ½ cup) sour cream or crème fraîche

1. Sauté the onions in butter, in covered frying pan until tender. Remove from heat.
2. Sift the flour and add baking powder and salt. Cut in the butter or shortening until you have a coarse cornmeal texture.
3. Add the milk and parsley and mix together until it is well blended.
4. Turn flour mixture into a well-greased 8-inch (20 cm) square baking pan. Top with onions and spoon the sour cream or crème fraîche over it.
5. Bake in preheated hot oven at 425°F (210°C) for 20-25 minutes or until lightly browned on top. Cut into 9 squares and serve.

Serves 4-5

Fried Onion Rings

*These onion rings, infinitely better than most restaurant ones,
should be eaten immediately as they do not keep well in the oven.*

vegetable oil for deep frying
4 very large onions, thinly sliced
3 cups flour
salt and pepper

1. Pour vegetable oil at least 2 inches (5 cm) deep into a large
   saucepan. Heat to a temperature of 375°F (190°C).
2. Separate onion slices into rings.
3. Spoon flour into a bag. Put a handful of rings at a time into the
   bag and shake it to coat rings. Then shake rings to take off
   excess flour.
4. Drop floured rings in the oil, not too many at a time. Cook for
   about 4 minutes, stirring occasionally.
5. When they are golden brown, take a slotted spoon and remove
   them from the oil. Drain on paper towels, season, and serve.

Serves 4

Spanish Onion Omelette

A Spanish omelette, or tortilla, *is cooked on both sides, not folded, and cut into wedges to serve while the center is still soft. It is good served hot or cold, in a sandwich, or as an hors d'oeuvre.*

2 medium Spanish onions
2 tablespoons olive oil
4 eggs
salt and pepper

1. Peel and thinly slice the onions. Heat the oil in a pan and fry onions slowly until they are golden. Season.
2. Beat the eggs and add more seasoning. Pour over the onions, covering them completely and evenly. Turn over to cook on the other side.
3. If you are nervous about breaking the omelette when you turn it over, try turning the pan over onto another hot slightly larger and greased frying pan. Or slip it onto a large plate; then, holding pan upside down over plate, turn them both over so that omelette falls into pan.

Serves 4-6

Caramelized Onions with Lentils and Rice

This Middle Eastern meal is a rare offering for lunch or a treat on the vegetarian supper menu.

3 tablespoons olive oil
1 medium onion, chopped
2 medium onions, halved and sliced
2-3 cloves garlic, minced
1 teaspoon ground cumin
salt and freshly ground black pepper to taste
1 lb (450 g or 2 cups) lentils
48 fl oz (about 1½ litres or 6 cups) stock (chicken, beef, or vegetable)
8 oz (225 g or 1 cup) rice
chopped parsley for garnish

1. Heat 1 tablespoon of the oil in a large saucepan for a minute. Add the chopped onion and cook until tender, about 5 minutes. Add the garlic, cumin, salt and pepper. Cook for another 3 minutes. Add the washed lentils and mix together. Stir in about two thirds of the stock.
2. Simmer, stirring occasionally, for about 20 minutes, until lentils begin to soften. Keep adding enough of the remaining stock to keep lentils covered by about an inch of liquid.
3. Stir in the rice. Cover and continue cooking on low heat.
4. While it is cooking, prepare caramelized onions. Place the remaining oil in a frying pan on medium-high heat. Add the onion slices and cook for about 15 minutes, stirring frequently to keep them from burning. When they are dark brown and nicely caramelized, remove them from pan with a slotted spoon and drain them on paper towels until lentil and rice mixture is done.

5. The cooking is done when liquid is absorbed and lentils and rice are tender. If more cooking time is needed, add more liquid and cook with lid on a bit longer. If rice and lentils are tender but too much liquid remains, continue to cook over raised heat and stir until liquid evaporates.
6. Turn rice and lentils into a serving bowl. Top with the caramelized onions and garnish with parsley and serve.

Serves 8-10

Stuffed Onions

A great way to use up those large garden onions, as well as a bit of leftover protein, and make a pleasant luncheon repast.

6 large onions
4 tablespoons butter
½ green pepper, chopped
8 oz (225g) mushrooms or 8 oz (225g) cooked meat, poultry, or fish
8 oz (225g) cooked rice or mashed potatoes
salt and pepper
soy sauce or curry powder or a seasoning of your choice
4 tablespoons fine bread crumbs or grated Parmesan cheese
butter to dot

1. Peel onions leaving root ends uncut and leaving onions whole. Cut a thick slice off the top of each. Boil onions together with the top slices until tender, about 30 minutes. Drain and cool. Spoon out central portion to form cups, leaving ½ inch (1.2 cm) walls. Save the centers and turn the cups over to drain.
2. Heat 2 tablespoons butter in a frying pan, and add the chopped green pepper and the mushrooms or other stuffing, cut up into small dice. Cook for a minute or two.
3. Add the cooked rice or mashed potatoes, the seasonings, and chopped onion from the tops and centers (as much as you like). Stuff the onion shells with this mixture.
4. Sprinkle the tops with bread crumbs or cheese and with knobs of butter.
5. Place in a pan, adding just enough water to cover the bottom. Bake until top is browned, about 20-30 minutes.

Serves 6

Parsnips

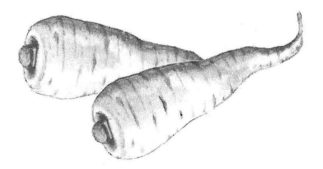

PARSNIPS

Parsnips are best from October onwards, before the central core becomes woody. Avoid the hard core of very large parsnips and use small ones, about four to six per pound. The lovely sweet flavor of parsnips, even sweeter than carrots, is improved by a touch of frost.

This minimum-care vegetable offers many appetizing methods of preparation, but mere boiling can be boring. Parsnips can be mashed or puréed, made into soup, added to casseroles or stews, or cut into thin strips and deep-fried like potatoes.

Perhaps the simplest way to use them is to cook them in boiling water until tender, then add melted butter and salt and pepper. Or sauté thinly-sliced parsnips in butter over medium heat until they are tender and brown. Raw parsnips make a good salad and can be used like cabbage (in coleslaw) or like carrots (perhaps with raisins). Indeed, parsnips can be used in any recipe for cooked carrots.

This sweet-tasting root was used in puddings and desserts in medieval times. Parsnips are still roasted around a joint of meat, as in days before the potato arrived from the New World.

Parsnips have a long shelf life and can keep for weeks or even months. If you have a large crop, try freezing them by peeling and cutting into quarters, slices, or cubes. Blanch for 2 minutes, cool and drain, and pack in containers or freezer bags.

RECIPES for PARSNIPS

Cream of Parsnip Soup

*The sweet but earthy flavor of parsnips blends well with the
simple ingredients that go into this soup recipe.*

2 tablespoons butter
1 large leek, chopped
3-4 parsnips, peeled and sliced
1 stalk celery, sliced
1 small-medium potato, diced
32 fl oz (900 ml) chicken broth
salt and freshly ground pepper to taste
8 oz (225 ml or 1 cup) light or single cream

1. Melt the butter in a large pot and sauté the leeks until soft.
2. Add parsnips, celery, potato, broth, salt and pepper. Cover pot
   and bring to a boil. Then reduce heat and simmer with cover
   on until vegetables are tender, about 20 minutes.
3. Purée in a food processor or blender.
4. Return to pot over gentle heat and stir in the cream. Correct
   seasoning and heat before serving.

Serves 6-8

Curried Parsnip Soup

*This thick and delectably flavored soup, with a velvety texture,
can also be made using vegetable instead of chicken stock*

1 lb (500 g) parsnips
2 tablespoons butter
1 medium onion, chopped
6 spring onions (or 2 leeks)
1 stalk celery, sliced
1 teaspoon curry powder
32 fl oz (1 litre or 4 cups) chicken stock
1 teaspoon salt
¼ teaspoon white pepper
1 tablespoon parsley
4 fl oz (100 ml or ½ cup) cream
yogurt
fresh coriander leaves to garnish

1. Heat butter in a large saucepan and sauté onion and spring onions until golden. Add sliced celery, chopped parsnips, and curry powder. Cook for a further 2 minutes.
2. Add stock, salt and pepper, and parsley. Simmer covered for an additional 30 minutes or until tender.
3. Cool slightly, then purée in a blender or food processor.
4. Reheat in a saucepan but do not boil. Stir in cream and adjust seasonings.
5. Serve topped with a spoonful of yogurt and chopped coriander leaves to garnish.

Serves 6

Chunky Parsnip Chowder

This can be prepared in advance by completing the first two steps. When ready to serve, follow the third step—and enjoy.

2 tablespoons butter
1 medium onion, coarsely chopped
3 medium-large parsnips (about 3 cups), peeled and cut into
small cubes
1 medium potato, peeled and cut into small cubes
2 medium carrots, peeled and cut into small cubes
16 fl oz (450 ml or 2 cups) water
1 teaspoon salt
freshly ground black pepper, to taste
12 fl oz (325 ml or 1½ cups) milk
8 fl oz (225 ml or 1 cup) light or single cream
1 tablespoon butter

1. Measure 2 tablespoons butter into a large pot. Add the onion and sauté over low to medium heat until soft.
2. Add the parsnips, potatoes, carrots, water, salt, and pepper. Cover pot and bring to a boil. Then reduce heat and simmer until vegetables are tender, about 10 to 12 minutes.
3. Stir in milk, cream and 1 tablespoon butter. Heat gently before serving but do not allow it to boil.

Serves 8

Parsnip Apple Salad

*Apples with red skin will add colour to this simple salad, which
looks and tastes like Waldorf salad. But guests may find it
difficult to identify parsnips as the mystery ingredient.*

1 lb (500 g) peeled and shredded parsnips
2 medium apples, unpeeled and coarsely chopped
1-2 stalks celery, chopped
4 oz (100 g or ½ cup) chopped walnuts
4 tablespoons oil and vinegar dressing
4 tablespoons mayonnaise (or less)
salt and pepper to taste

1. Mix together the parsnips, apples, celery, and walnuts with
   the oil and vinegar dressing.
2. Stir in only enough mayonnaise to moisten the salad. Season
   with salt and pepper and blend.
3. Chill for at least 1 hour before serving.

Serves 6-8

Parsnip Purée

A staple winter vegetable, parsnips are often served mashed or puréed. Use as many as you like in this basic recipe, which can be prepared in advance.

parsnips
carrots or pumpkin (optional)
butter
nutmeg
fresh chopped parsley
freshly ground black pepper
a little cream or cooking liquid, if needed

1. Prepare parsnips by cutting off roots and tops, then peel. Cut into slices. If mature, cut into quarters and remove the hard core.
2. Steam for 20-30 minutes or until they can be easily pierced with a skewer. Add carrot or pumpkin if you want to. Drain.
3. Purée in a food processor with a little butter, nutmeg, chopped parsley, and freshly ground black pepper until the mixture is smooth. Use liquid if needed.
4. You can prepare the recipe in advance stopping at this point if you want to. Place purée in a covered bowl in the refrigerator for up to two days before serving. When ready, reheat and serve.

Parsnip and Pear Purée

An unusual side dish, this sweet-tasting and easily-made purée goes well with roasted meat, poultry, or game.

2 lbs (900 g) parsnips, sliced
1 lb (450 g) ripe pears, peeled and quartered
5 tablespoons sour cream
salt and pepper to taste

1. Cook the parsnips until soft, about 25 minutes. Add the pears and cook for a further 5 minutes. When both are soft, drain.
2. Blend the mixture into a purée using a food processor or blender and add sour cream and salt and pepper.
3. Serve. Or transfer the purée to an ovenproof dish and heat up when you are ready.

Serves 6-8

Candied Parsnips

Dress up your parsnips with the pleasing and palatable taste given in this recipe.

6 parsnips
3-4 oz (100g or ½ cup) brown sugar (or less, depending on taste)
salt, to taste
4 fl oz (100 ml or ½ cup) orange juice
1 teaspoon grated orange rind
3-4 tablespoons butter

1. Boil peeled parsnips in a saucepan for about 20 minutes, or until almost tender. Remove them from saucepan and cut into slices.
2. In a greased casserole, arrange the parsnip slices in layers, sprinkling each layer with brown sugar, salt, orange juice, orange rind, and dots of butter.
3. Bake in a preheated oven at 375°F (190°C) for about 30 minutes.

Serves 6

Parsnip Curry

A perfect accompaniment for perking up a simple meal.

1 small-medium onion, chopped
1 tablespoon olive oil
½ teaspoon cumin
1 teaspoon chili powder
1½ teaspoons turmeric
½ teaspoon cayenne pepper
½ teaspoon salt
1 lb (450 g) parsnips, peeled and diced
4 fl oz (110 ml or ½ cup) water
half a green pepper, cut into thin strips
2 oz (50 g) peanuts, chopped

1. In a large saucepan, sauté onion in oil until golden, about 5 minutes.
2. Add spices and seasonings. Stir and cook for 1 minute.
3. Add diced parsnips and water. Bring to a boil, then cover and simmer over low heat until parsnips are tender, about 20 minutes. Taste for seasonings, and increase amount of cayenne if you want a spicier dish.
4. Garnish with pepper strips and peanuts when ready to serve.

Serves 4-6

Parsnip and Carrot Ragout

*Parsnips and carrots go well together, and this vegetable dish
has the advantage that it can be prepared in advance to avoid
last-minute bustle for a dinner party.*

4 medium-large parsnips
4 medium carrots
2 oz (50 g) butter
1 onion, finely sliced
1 clove garlic, finely chopped
5 fl oz (150 ml) chicken stock
salt and freshly ground black pepper

1. Peel the parsnips and carrots, and cut both into fine strips.
2. Melt butter in a fireproof casserole and cook the sliced onion
   over low heat until it is soft.
3. Add the chopped garlic and the parsnips and carrots. Cook for
   2-3 minutes, stirring occasionally until vegetables are coated
   with butter. Pour on the stock and add salt and freshly ground
   black pepper.
4. Cover and simmer gently for about 40 minutes.

Serves 6

Parsnip-Tomato Casserole

With its friendly combination of parsnips, tomatoes, cheese and cream, this casserole goes well with any number of main meat courses, especially roast lamb and beef.

2 lbs (1 kg) parsnips
1 lb (450 g) tomatoes
5 tablespoons oil
3 oz (75 g) butter
3 tablespoons brown sugar
salt and freshly ground black pepper
6 oz (175 g) Gruyère cheese, grated
10 fl oz (300 ml or ½ pint) cream
4 tablespoons fresh white breadcrumbs

1. Peel the parsnips and slice them thinly, cutting away any hard core.
2. Skin the tomatoes and cut them into slices.
3. Heat the oil in a pan and fry parsnips lightly for about 4-5 minutes.
4. Grease a casserole with half the butter, and arrange a layer of parsnips over the bottom. Sprinkle with a little sugar, salt and pepper. Add a little cream and a layer of tomatoes. Add a little more cream and cheese over the tomatoes and repeat these layers until all the ingredients are used up, ending with cream and cheese. Finally, sprinkle breadcrumbs over the top and dot with remaining butter.
5. Place casserole in an oven preheated to 325°F (170°C) for 40 minutes.

Serves 6

Parsnip-Potato-Pecan Casserole

This triple-P casserole makes a great company dish, whether served as an accompaniment or as a main course with a salad.

5 parsnips, diced
3 tablespoons butter
1 onion, diced
4 fl oz (150 ml or ½ cup) cream
4 oz (150 ml or ½ cup) natural yogurt
1 tablespoon tamari (soy sauce)
pepper to taste
2 lbs (1 kg) potatoes, cooked and sliced
4-6 oz (110-170 g) pecans, roughly chopped
butter for topping

1. Heat butter in a frying pan and sauté onion with parsnips until they begin to soften. Add cream, yogurt, tamari, and pepper. Cook until tender, about 10 minutes. Remove from heat.
2. Boil and slice potatoes. Place a layer of potatoes in the bottom of a lightly-buttered casserole, then half the parsnip mixture, followed by another layer of potatoes, and the remaining parsnips, then pecans, ending with potatoes. Dot the top with butter.
3. Bake in a 350°F (180°C) oven for about 40 minutes.

Serves 6-8

Parsnip Pancakes

Similar to potato pancakes, these patties are an absolutely delicious way of preparing this root vegetable. You can prepare the parsnip mixture as much as a day ahead of time and fry just before serving.

4 small parsnips (about 12 oz or 350 g), grated or finely shredded
2 tablespoons chopped onion
2 eggs, beaten
8 tablespoons flour
1 tablespoon butter, melted
2 fl oz (50 ml or ¼ cup) milk
½ teaspoon salt
1/8 teaspoon freshly ground pepper
1-2 tablespoons oil

1. Place all the ingredients except the oil in a large bowl and mix thoroughly.
2. Heat oil in a large frying pan over medium heat. Drop the parsnip mixture into pan by spoonfuls and flatten them with back of spoon into 2-inch (5 cm) patties.
3. Fry until brown, turning over once until the other side is brown (about 5 minutes each side).

Serves 6-8

Parsnip Sour Cream Muffins

The sour cream makes these muffins moist and luscious, but no one will guess that parsnips are the secret ingredient. Use less sugar if your parsnips are particularly sweet.

1 egg, beaten
4 oz (110 ml or ½ cup) sour cream
2 parsnips (about 10 oz or 290 g), cooked and well-mashed
2 tablespoons butter, melted
3 fl oz (75 ml or 1/3 cup) milk
8 oz (230 g or 1½ cups) flour, sifted
4 oz (120 g or ½ cup) sugar—or less
1½ teaspoons baking powder
½ teaspoon baking soda
½ teaspoon salt
½ teaspoon cinnamon
¼ teaspoon nutmeg
¼ teaspoon ginger
1/8 teaspoon cloves
chopped pecans (optional)
sugar and cinnamon for topping (optional)

1. Put the egg, sour cream, mashed parsnip, butter, and milk in a bowl and mix well.
2. Add the dry ingredients to the egg mixture and stir together to make a thick batter. Mix in the chopped pecans if desired.
3. Spoon batter into a greased muffin tin. Sprinkle with sugar or cinnamon if you want to.
4. Bake in preheated oven at 400°F (200°C) for about 20-25 minutes.

Makes 12-14 muffins

Parsnip Pie

Try this instead of pumpkin pie during the autumnal harvest season. Use more spice if you like, and use less sugar if your parsnips are on the sweeter side.

9-inch unbaked pie shell
2 eggs
14 fl oz (400 ml or 1¾ cups) light or single cream
12 oz (340 g or 1½ cups) peeled, cooked and puréed parsnips
3 oz (75 g) brown sugar
3 oz (75 g) sugar
½ teaspoon salt
1¼ teaspoons cinnamon
¼ teaspoon nutmeg
¼ teaspoon ginger
whipped cream (optional)

1. Measure all the ingredients into a large bowl. Using an electric mixer, beat them all together at low speed until well blended.
2. Brush inside of pie shell with lightly beaten egg white and pour mixture into the shell.
3. Bake in a hot oven preheated to 400°F (200°C) until it is set, about 50-55 minutes
4. Serve at room temperature. Or top with whipped cream and serve chilled.

Parsnip and Ginger Cake

If you like ginger, you will like this unusual tea bread which uses both fresh and preserved ginger and may be served warm, spread with butter. (You may also use grated carrots or courgettes in place of parsnips.)

3 eggs
8 oz (225 g or 1 cup) sugar
8 fl oz (250 ml or 1 cup) sunflower oil
1 teaspoon vanilla extract
1 tablespoon syrup from jar of preserved stem ginger
2-3 small parsnips (8 oz or 225 g), grated
1 inch (2.5 cm) piece of fresh root ginger, grated
12 oz (350 g or 2½ cups) plain flour
1 teaspoon (5 ml) baking powder
pinch of salt
1 teaspoon cinnamon
2 pieces preserved stem ginger, chopped
1 tablespoon brown sugar

1. Beat eggs and sugar together until fluffy. Beat in the oil slowly. Add the vanilla and ginger syrup. Stir in the grated parsnips and ginger and blend it all together.
2. Sift flour into a large bowl and add baking powder, salt, and cinnamon. Then stir the dry ingredients into the parsnip mixture and blend well.
3. Turn the batter into a lightly greased loaf tin. Smooth the top and sprinkle it with the chopped stem ginger and brown sugar.
4. Bake in an oven preheated to 325°F (190°C) for about 1 hour or until a skewer inserted into the center comes out clean. When ready to serve cut into slices.

Potatoes

POTATOES

The potato is the most popular of all vegetables and justifies an entire book of recipes on its own. Nevertheless, of the myriad methods of using potatoes, this selection of less usual—but easy to prepare—recipes will go some way toward increasing your repertory and decreasing your crop.

Freshly dug new potatoes are exquisite enough to be cooked plain, perhaps with the addition of butter and a little bit of chives or mint. They really do not need fancy recipes. Or, warm some sliced cooked new potatoes in a little melted butter, add a mixture of 4 tablespoons cream and 2 tablespoons French mustard, and cook together for about 5 minutes. Fantastic with fish or chicken!

Furthermore, contrary to popular belief, they are not devoid of nutritional value but are rich in vitamins (particularly Vitamin C) and potassium, with the part just under the skin richest in nutrients. And they are low in calories when eaten plain. Potatoes have no fat and are very satisfying and filling.

There are literally hundreds of varieties of potatoes, but only fifteen are in general use. Early potatoes are best boiled, chipped, roasted, or used in salads. Maincrop potatoes may be baked, roasted, mashed, chipped, or used in salads or soups. For additional soup recipes see Vichyssoise (page 101) and Spanish Onion and Potato Soup (page 123).

RECIPES for POTATOES

SOUPS

SALADS

ACCOMPANIMENTS

MAIN MEALS

Asparagus Potato Soup

A superb variation on the usual leek-and-potato soup theme.

1 lb (450 g) asparagus
3 medium potatoes (1 lb or 450 g), peeled and diced
1 small onion, sliced
3 sprigs parsley
24 fl oz (650 ml or 3 cups) water
salt and pepper
1 bouillon cube or 1 teaspoon powdered chicken soup mix

1. Wash asparagus and cut into 2-inch (5 cm) lengths, discarding the tough lower parts of the stalks.
2. Place all the ingredients in a large saucepan and bring to a boil, then simmer covered for about 15-20 minutes, until the vegetables are tender.
3. Transfer to a food processor and purée the mixture.
4. Serve hot. Or place in refrigerator and serve cold.

Serves 6-8

Creamy Potato Soup

Make ahead and serve cold, or reheat and serve warm.

3 medium potatoes (1 lb or 450 g), peeled and thinly sliced
12 fl oz (350 ml or 1½ cups) chicken broth
8 fl oz (225 ml or 1 cup) skim milk
1 tablespoon butter
2-3 spring onions (scallions), thinly sliced
2 tablespoons fresh chopped parsley
½ teaspoon celery seed
¼ teaspoon tarragon
salt and pepper to taste

1. Place potatoes and broth in a saucepan and bring to a boil. Cook, covered, until potatoes are tender, about 10 minutes. Stir occasionally and add more liquid if necessary. Cool slightly.
2. Blend in a food processor until smooth and pour back into saucepan.
3. Mix in milk, butter, and sliced spring onions. Add remaining ingredients.
4. Bring to a boil and serve warm. Or chill and serve cold. Thin with a little extra milk if necessary.

Serves 4

Cold Curried Potato Soup

A refreshing soup, especially on a hot summer evening.

3 medium potatoes (1 lb or 450 g)
16 fl oz (450 ml or 2 cups) water
¾ teaspoon cumin
¼ teaspoon ground ginger
½ teaspoon turmeric
1/8 teaspoon nutmeg
¼ teaspoon celery seed
½ teaspoon mustard seed
1 large onion, chopped
1 tablespoon butter
salt and pepper
cayenne pepper
1 tablespoon fresh lemon juice
8 oz (225 ml or 1 cup) yogurt

1. Peel potatoes and slice them very thinly. Put them into a large saucepan with the water, cover, and bring to a boil. Reduce heat and simmer about 10-15 minutes until potatoes are tender, being careful not to overcook. Remove from heat.
2. Mix together the cumin, ginger, turmeric, nutmeg, celery seed, and mustard seed.
3. In a frying pan, sauté the onions in butter for several minutes over medium heat. Stir in the spice mixture. Add salt and pepper and cayenne to taste. Continue cooking and stirring for another 5 minutes or until onions are tender.
4. Combine sautéed onion mixture with potatoes in a food processor or blender and process until smooth. Add lemon juice and mix well. Chill.
5. Shortly before serving, stir in yogurt.

Serves 4-5

Watercress and Potato Soup

Also known by the fancier name of Potage Cresson, this soup has a subtle and delicious taste to match its elegant name.

1 small onion, chopped
1 tablespoon vegetable oil
1 large bunch watercress, chopped
3 medium potatoes (1 lb or 450 g), peeled and cubed
40 fl oz (1.2 litres or 5 cups) chicken stock
1 teaspoon salt
dash of white pepper
dash of nutmeg
6 oz (175 ml or ¾ cup) milk
1-2 tablespoons butter (optional)

1. In a large saucepan, sauté the onion in oil over low heat until the onion is soft, about 5-10 minutes.
2. Add the watercress and continue to sauté for just another few minutes.
3. Add the potatoes, water, soup mix or bouillon cubes, salt and pepper, and nutmeg. Bring to a boil, then simmer over low heat, covered, about 15 minutes or until potatoes are soft.
4. Purée mixture in a food processor or blender.
5. When ready to serve, bring the purée to the boiling point. Blend in the milk, and bring it to the boiling point again. If you want to, stir in a few tablespoons of butter for more richness. Serve.

Serves 8

Potato Salad

Allowing the flavors to blend by preparing it the day before it is needed will make this salad even better.

3 lbs (1.4 kg) potatoes
6 tablespoons dry white wine
5 tablespoons oil
2½ tablespoons red wine vinegar
½ teaspoon salt
¼ teaspoon pepper
4 tablespoons mayonnaise
4 tablespoons chopped spring onions or Spanish onions
4 tablespoons chopped fresh parsley

1. In a saucepan, cook the unpeeled potatoes in boiling water until they are tender, about 20-30 minutes. They should be firm and not overcooked.
2. Drain. While they are still warm, peel and cut the potatoes into ¾ inch (1.9 cm) cubes.
3. Drizzle the white wine over them and allow to stand for 10 minutes.
4. Using a whisk, beat together the oil, vinegar, salt and pepper. Add this dressing to the potatoes, and mix together gently. Refrigerate overnight at this stage, if you want to.
5. Remove any remaining liquid. Add mayonnaise, onions, and parsley. Gently mix together.

Serves 8

Broccoli Potato Salad

A welcome change from ordinary potato salad, this healthy recipe is a favorite of mine.

6 medium new potatoes (about 2 lbs or 1 kg)
1½-2 cups fresh broccoli florets (cut from half a large stalk)
2 fl oz (50 ml or ¼ cup) orange juice
3 tablespoons olive oil
3 tablespoons white wine vinegar
2 teaspoons basil
1-2 cloves garlic, minced
¼ teaspoon hot pepper sauce
2 tablespoons fresh chopped parsley
2 spring onions, thinly sliced
salt to taste

1. Cut potatoes into 1-inch (2.5 cm) cubes and cook until just tender, about 15 minutes. Drain.
2. Blanch broccoli in boiling water for 1 minute. Drain and combine with potatoes.
3. Combine juice, oil, vinegar, basil and garlic in a saucepan and bring to a boil. Remove from heat and stir in pepper sauce. Pour the mixture over potatoes and broccoli.
4. Add parsley, spring onions, and salt. Toss gently with a wooden spoon and serve warm. Alternatively, place in the refrigerator to chill and serve cold.

Serves 8

Mashed Potato Variations

Mashed potatoes, a perennial favorite, are compatible with so many partners. The basic recipe given here is followed by a few ways to vary mashed potatoes, just to avoid any possibility of boredom—and take advantage of your potato supply.

4 medium potatoes
2 tablespoons butter
a little milk or yogurt or crème fraiche
salt and pepper to taste

1. Place potatoes, peeled and cut into pieces, into a pot of boiling salted water and cook until tender. Drain thoroughly.
2. Mash the potatoes well until there are no lumps. Beat in the butter and milk or yogurt or crème fraiche. Season with salt and pepper.

Serves 4

Variations:

Green Onions: Add 2-3 oz (50-75 g) minced green onions to the mashed potatoes.

Mushrooms: Sauté ½ lb (225 g) sliced mushrooms in 2 tablespoons butter and add to mashed potatoes.

Olive Oil: Cook 2lbs (1 kg) potatoes and mash them on their own. In a saucepan, heat 6 fl oz (75 ml) olive oil, 6 oz (75 ml) heavy or double cream, and 1 crushed garlic clove. Beat the mixture with a whisk and add salt and cayenne pepper to taste. Slowly flow the mixture into the warm potatoes and blend it all together. It may be kept warm in the oven.

Cheese: Remove the mashed potatoes to a buttered heatproof serving platter, spreading them evenly about 2 inches (5 cm) thick. Sprinkle grated cheese over the top and brush with melted butter. Place under broiler to brown.

Orange: Sauté a large chopped onion in butter until tender. Stir it into the mashed potatoes. Stir in 4 oz (100 ml or ½ cup) crème fraîche or yogurt and 6 oz (175 ml or ¾ cup) orange juice and beat with a whisk until fluffy. Spoon into a serving dish and garnish with grated orange rind.

Cornflakes: Form mashed potatoes into balls. Dilute 1 beaten egg with 2 tablespoons water. Roll potato balls in egg, then in crushed cornflakes. Place on greased baking sheet and bake in preheated oven at 375°F (190°C) until heated through, about 15-20 minutes.

Egg Luncheon Dish: Grease individual muffin cups and fill with hot mashed potatoes, making a depression in the top of each. Drop an egg in each depression. Bake in a preheated moderate oven at 375°F (190°C) until eggs are set.

Baked Stuffed Potatoes

The thing I like about these stuffed potatoes, apart from the excellent taste, is their convenience as party fare. They can be made ahead of time and reheated or put in the freezer and taken out for reheating. Double or triple the recipe, as required.

6 large potatoes, baked
2 oz (50 g) butter
2 egg yolks
4 oz (125 g) grated cheese
salt and freshly ground black pepper
1-2 tablespoons finely chopped fresh parsley

1. Cut each baked potato in half lengthwise and with a spoon carefully scoop out the pulp into a bowl, leaving a ¼ inch (.6 cm) shell.
2. Mash potatoes thoroughly, then beat in the butter, egg yolks, grated cheese, seasoning and parsley. Fill the potato shells with this mixture. Score the potato mound with the prongs of a fork to make an attractive look.
3. When ready to serve, place the potato halves (defrosted if necessary) on a baking tray and bake for 30-40 minutes in a preheated oven at 350°F (180°C).

Serves 12

NOTE:
As an alternative, change the ingredients in step 2 by beating into the potatoes butter, yogurt, lemon juice, dill weed, garlic powder, salt and pepper. Sprinkle the filled potato shells with paprika.

New Potatoes with Sour Cream-Dill Dressing

Here is a good-natured way to enhance newly harvested potatoes.

2 lbs (1 kg) new potatoes
6 fl oz (175 g or ¾ cup) sour cream
white pepper to taste
½ teaspoon dill seed

1. Wash the potatoes and put them into a saucepan with just enough boiling salted water to almost cover them.
2. With lid on, simmer over medium heat for about 20-25 minutes, shaking the pan from time to time, until they are done but still firm. Drain, remove lid, and cook a bit longer to allow any remaining water to evaporate.
3. Mix together the sour cream, pepper, and dill seed. Toss the mixture gently with the potatoes and serve.

Serves 6

New Potatoes with Mint

Young new potatoes are so delicious that I offer another easy method of preparing them. Enjoy the wonderful aroma and taste!

2 lbs (1 kg) new potatoes
1 sprig fresh mint
1½ oz (40 g) butter
2 tablespoon chopped fresh mint
1 tablespoon fresh cut chives
1 tablespoon chopped fresh parsley
pepper

1. Wash the potatoes and put them in a saucepan with enough boiling salted water to almost cover them. Add the sprig of mint. Cover and simmer for about 20-25 minutes, until they are tender but firm. Drain.
2. Mix the butter together with the herbs and pepper, and add the mixture to the drained potatoes. Place the lid back on the saucepan and shake the pan around to coat each potato. Transfer to a serving dish.

Serves 6

Potatoes in Wine

This splendid way of serving potatoes makes for a welcome and wonderful change.

1 lb (450 g) potatoes, cut into ½ inch (1.2 cm) cubes
8 fl oz (225 ml or 1 cup) dry white wine
2 fl oz (50 ml or ¼ cup) white wine vinegar
2 spring onions, thinly sliced
1 clove garlic, minced
½ teaspoon basil
pinch of pepper
1 teaspoon Dijon mustard
1 tablespoon chopped fresh basil or parsley

1. Wash potatoes and cut them into cubes.
2. Place them in a saucepan with the white wine, wine vinegar, spring onions, garlic, basil, and pepper. Bring to a boil, then reduce heat and simmer until potatoes are tender, about 25 minutes.
3. Using a slotted spoon, take the potatoes out of the saucepan and place them in a warm serving bowl. Reserve the liquid and keep the potatoes warm.
4. Cook the reserved liquid, stirring from time to time, until it is reduced and thickened. Mix in the mustard and drip this mixture over the potatoes. Garnish with basil or parsley and serve.

Serves 4

Moroccan Potatoes

The yellowish color which comes from the turmeric combines with the olives to make an attractive presentation—and a delectable dish.

2 lbs (1 kg) small new potatoes
½ teaspoon turmeric
4 garlic cloves, minced
4 tablespoons olive oil
salt and pepper to taste
4 oz (100 g) black or Nicoise olives
1 small bunch of coriander leaves, coarsely chopped

1. Cook the small potatoes (or larger ones, cut up) in water with the turmeric. When the potatoes are tender, after about 10 minutes, drain and place them in a baking dish together with the garlic, olive oil, salt and pepper, and olives. Mix it all together.
2. Bake in a preheated oven at 350°F (180°C) for 30 minutes. Scatter chopped coriander over the top and serve.

Serves 6

Potatoes with Lentils

Lentils, both nutritious and delicious, combine well with potatoes for a dish that makes a good side accompaniment.

1 large potato or 2 medium, cut into cubes
8 oz (225 g) lentils
½ teaspoon salt
1 tablespoon olive oil
2 cloves garlic, minced
small onion or shallot, chopped
freshly ground black pepper
pinch of cumin (optional)

1. Peel potatoes, cut into small cubes, and place in a saucepan.
2. Wash lentils and add them to potatoes in the saucepan. Add salt and cover with water.
3. Bring to a boil, then reduce heat, cover and simmer until vegetables are tender, about 20-25 minutes. Drain.
4. Measure olive oil into a frying pan and sauté the garlic and onion.
5. Spoon the lentils and potatoes into this mixture. Stir it all together over moderate heat, adding pepper to taste and cumin if you want to, and serve.

Serves 6

Italian Potato Soufflé

*Refrigerate or freeze this elegant party casserole. When ready to
serve, bring to room temperature and bake.*

**3 lbs (1.4 kg) potatoes
3 eggs, beaten
3 tablespoons Parmesan cheese
freshly ground black pepper to taste
about 8 oz (225 g) mozzarella cheese, sliced
buttered crumbs
freshly chopped parsley**

1. Boil the potatoes and mash well. Beat in eggs. Add Parmesan
   cheese and pepper and blend thoroughly.
2. In a lightly-buttered casserole, alternate layers of potatoes and
   sliced mozzarella cheese.
3. Top with buttered crumbs and parsley.
4. Bake in oven preheated to 375°F (190°C) for 45 minutes.

Serves 8-10

Indian Spiced Potatoes

A golden spicy sauce gives this dish a luscious look and a pleasantly piquant flavor. For a finishing touch, sprinkle with fresh chopped coriander.

2 lbs (1 kg) potatoes
1 onion, chopped
2 tablespoons oil
1-2 garlic cloves, crushed
1 teaspoon turmeric
1 teaspoon ground coriander
1 teaspoon cumin
2 cardamom pods
5 fl oz (150 ml) water
salt and freshly ground black pepper
½ teaspoon chili powder (optional)
chopped coriander leaves (optional)

1. Peel potatoes and cut into ½ inch (1cm) dice.
2. Fry the onion in the oil for about 6-8 minutes. Add the garlic, turmeric, coriander, cumin, and cardamom. Cook and stir for another 2-3 minutes.
3. Add potatoes, turning gently to coat with the spice mixture. Add the water and salt and pepper. Add chili powder if you want to. Bring to a boil.
4. Cover and simmer over low heat for about 8-10 minutes, until the potatoes are just tender. Shake the pan or stir gently from time to time to prevent sticking.
5. Check seasonings. Garnish with chopped coriander and serve immediately.

Serves 6

Potatoes with Garlic and Lemon

Choose fairly large potatoes for this dish, if possible.

2 lbs (1 kg) potatoes, thickly sliced lengthways
olive oil
salt and pepper
grated rind of 1 large or 2 small lemons
2-3 cloves garlic, finely chopped
milk

1. Lightly coat potato slices in oil and arrange them, slightly overlapping in a buttered baking dish. Sprinkle each layer with salt and pepper, grated lemon rind and chopped garlic.
2. Add just enough milk to reach the top layer.
3. Bake in hot oven preheated to 400°F (200°C) until top layer is golden brown, about 30 minutes.

Serves 6

Greek Potatoes

These potatoes, appetizing and aromatic, may also be sprinkled with feta cheese.

3 lbs (1½ kg) potatoes, cut into cubes
2 lemons, freshly squeezed
3 fl oz (75 ml) olive oil
½ teaspoon black pepper
1 tablespoon oregano
2 garlic cloves, minced
24 fl oz (700 ml or 3 cups) hot water
chopped fresh parsley

1. Toss potatoes together with lemon juice, oil, pepper, oregano, and garlic. Place them in a deep flat pan about 8 x 12 inches (20 x 30 cm). Add water.
2. Bake uncovered for about 1½ hours at 425°F (220°C). Stir about every 20 minutes and add more water if necessary to prevent sticking. Be careful not to burn potatoes during the last 30 minutes. During the last 15-20 minutes allow water to evaporate until only oil is left.
3. Garnish with fresh parsley and serve.

Serves 8

Potato Latkes

The preparation of these pancakes, which are served as an appetizer or side dish, may be made easier by grating the potatoes and onion in a food processor. Latkes are a traditional dish in many Jewish homes especially during Hanukkah. The delicious end result justifies the effort.

about 3 lbs (1.4 k) potatoes, peeled and cut into cubes
1 medium-large onion, cut into quarters
2 eggs
1 teaspoon salt
1 teaspoon baking powder
¼ teaspoon pepper
2 tablespoons flour
3 tablespoons matzo meal
vegetable oil for frying

1. Grate the potatoes and onion in a food processor (or grate by hand), and drain in a colander or strainer. Place in bowl.
2. Beat the eggs lightly and mix them in. Add the remaining ingredients and stir well.
3. Heat a few tablespoons oil in a large frying pan. Drop the mixture by tablespoons into the hot oil. Flatten a little with the back of the spoon and fry until brown, then turn over and fry until golden brown on the other side. Add more oil as needed.
4. Lift out of pan and drain briefly on paper towels. Keep warm in the oven until all of them are done. Serve hot.

Serves 8-10

Potato Kugel

An excellent company dish that may be served as a first course or as a side dish to accompany meat or chicken.

2 lbs (1 kg) potatoes, peeled and grated
1 medium onion, grated
2 eggs, lightly beaten
4 tablespoons matzo meal
1 teaspoon baking powder
½ teaspoon salt
dash pepper

1. Grate the potatoes and drain them. Stir in all the other ingredients quickly to prevent potatoes from discoloring. Mix well.
2. Turn into a greased 8-inch (20.3 cm) square baking pan and bake at 350°F (180°C) for 35 minutes or until firm. Cut into squares and serve.

Serves 8

Potatoes À La Dauphinoise

Firm, waxy potatoes are essential for this great classic French dish, which makes a good accompaniment for roasts and poultry—or a meal on its own. Use Gruyère, Parmesan, or a robust cheese.

butter
2 lbs (1 k) potatoes, thinly sliced
4 oz (100 g) grated cheese
salt and pepper
grated nutmeg
1 egg
4 fl oz (100 ml) heavy cream

1. In a well-buttered baking dish, alternate layers of potatoes with a good sprinkling of cheese, and season each layer with salt and pepper and nutmeg.
2. Beat the egg and cream together and pour it over the potatoes. Finally, sprinkle cheese generously over the surface.
3. Bake in a moderate oven preheated to 325°F (160°C) for an hour, until potatoes are tender and the top is crisp with a rich golden color.

Serves 6

Anna Potatoes

Here is a classic dish of attractively-arranged potatoes that requires no last-minute fussing and can be left in a warm oven until you are ready.

6 large potatoes, thinly sliced
4-6 tablespoons butter
salt and freshly ground black pepper

1. Arrange the sliced potatoes in overlapping layers in a buttered baking dish. Sprinkle each layer with salt and pepper and dot with butter.
2. Cover with foil and bake in a 375°F (190°C) oven for 50-60 minutes. Then remove cover to color them a bit. (They can rest in a warm oven for a long while without spoiling.)

Serves 6

Boulangère Potatoes

The name of this classic French dish hearkens back to the good old days when people took their pots of potatoes to village bakeries to be cooked in bread ovens. It is an excellent choice for modern ovens and for dinner parties, as it needs no last minute attention.

2 lbs (900 g) potatoes, peeled and thinly sliced
1 large onion, chopped or a chopped leek
2 oz (50 g) butter
5 fl oz (150 ml) stock
5 fl oz (150 ml) milk
salt and freshly ground black pepper

1. In a well-buttered, oblong baking dish, arrange a layer of potato slices, then a sprinkling of onion (or leek) and salt and pepper. Continue arranging layers, finishing with potatoes.
2. Pour in the stock and milk. Dot the surface with remaining butter.
3. Bake in a preheated oven at 350°F (180°C) for about 40 minutes or until top layer is a deep golden color.

Serves 4-6

Potato Skins

This healthy version of those highly saturated potato skins often found in restaurants, is so delicious that it might take only two people to devour a recipe meant for six.

4 large potatoes
about 2 tablespoons olive oil
paprika to taste

1. Scrub potatoes well. Cut them lengthwise into six wedges in the shape of pickle spears. Pat them dry on a paper towel.
2. Toss potatoes with the olive oil in a large bowl until they are well coated.
3. Spread them on a baking sheet and sprinkle with paprika.
4. Bake in a preheated hot oven at 425°F (220°C) until they are tender when pierced with a fork, about 20-30 minutes.

Serves 6

Chili Potato Stew

This recipe makes a flavorful vegetarian main course, with the taste of chili and texture of shredded potatoes.

1½ tablespoons vegetable oil
1 medium-large onion, finely chopped
1 celery stalk, finely chopped
1 green pepper, finely chopped
4 cloves garlic, finely chopped
2 1-lb (450 g) cans tomatoes, undrained, chopped
2 1-lb (450 g) cans kidney beans, rinsed and drained
8 fl oz (225 ml or 1 cup) water
2 small-medium carrots, coarsely shredded
2 medium-large potatoes, coarsely shredded
1 tablespoon chili powder
1 tablespoon dried parsley flakes
1½ teaspoons dried oregano
1½ teaspoons dried basil
1 teaspoon ground cumin
1 teaspoon ground allspice
2 bay leaves
salt to taste

1. In a large pot, heat oil over medium heat. Add onions, celery, green pepper, and garlic. Cook about 10 minutes, stirring frequently, until vegetables are tender.
2. Add the rest of the ingredients and bring to a boil. Reduce heat and simmer covered for 1 hour, stirring occasionally. Remove bay leaves and serve.

Serves 8

Potatoes Cacciatore

*This Italian offering can be an accompaniment or an entrée.
Sprinkle it with Parmesan cheese if you like, and serve with a
salad.*

4 large potatoes (1½ lbs or 700 g)
1 tablespoon olive oil
1 medium onion, chopped
2 cloves garlic, minced
1 lb (450 g) can tomatoes, undrained and chopped (or fresh
  skinned tomatoes)
8 oz (225 ml) can tomato sauce
¼ teaspoon pepper
½ teaspoon dried oregano
½ teaspoon dried basil
½ teaspoon dried rosemary

1. Cut potatoes into ¼ inch (.6 cm) slices. Set aside.
2. Heat oil in a large frying pan over medium heat and cook onions and garlic in it, stirring frequently, until onions are tender, about 5 minutes. Remove from heat and add all remaining ingredients except potatoes. Mix well.
3. In a lightly-oiled 9x13-inch (23x31cm) baking pan, arrange a layer of potatoes. Spread half the tomato mixture evenly over the potatoes. Arrange another layer of potatoes and finish with the remaining tomato mixture. Cover tightly with aluminum foil.
4. Bake in preheated oven at 375°F (190°C) for 50 minutes.

Serves 6-8

Spanish Potato Omelet

Called a tortilla in Spain, where it is generally served as a first course, this classic Spanish dish may also be enjoyed as a main luncheon or supper course along with salad and bread. It may be eaten hot or cold and is perfect for a late supper or anytime snack.

1 lb (450 g) potatoes, peeled and thinly sliced
1 large onion, finely chopped
2-4 fl oz (50-100 ml) olive oil
4 eggs, beaten
salt and freshly ground black pepper

1. Heat olive oil in a large frying pan. Sauté onions until soft and golden. Add the potatoes and sauté until onion and potatoes have browned. Season with salt and pepper.
2. Pour the beaten eggs over the mixture. Continue cooking for about one minute.
3. When it is almost firm, hold a plate upside down over the frying pan; invert both, dropping the omelet onto the plate, then slip the omelet back into the pan, browned side up, allowing the bottom to brown. Serve immediately if you want a hot course, or allow to cool.

Serves 2-4

Radishes

RADISHES

Although they are the first root vegetable of spring and a harbinger of crops to come, radishes are available all year round. Numerous varieties of radishes make for a wide range of sizes, shapes, and colors. They may be round and red or tapering and white, or bright red with white tips or black with white flesh.

Radishes are generally served raw in salads, many of which can be quite unusual. But, yes, you can also cook radishes and turn them into quite delicious gastronomic treats. When cooked, radishes lose their familiar sharp flavor and take on a milder taste.

Radishes have so many uses: Slice them and add to stir fry mix. Trim leaves leaving a small bit of stalk as a handle and dip into mayonnaise or sauce. Cook in a splash of hot oil until they are tender and season to taste. Or simply add whole or halved or sliced radishes to any salad for that extra bite.

Garnish cold entrées, hors d'oeuvres, salads, etc. with radish roses by making 6-8 lengthways cuts through the radish from root end to stalk, about two thirds of the way down. Place in a bowl of ice water until they open up like roses.

RECIPES for RADISHES

SALADS

ACCOMPANIMENTS or SIDE DISHES

Russian Radish Salad

Traditionally, this salad calls for strong black or purple winter radishes, but other radishes may also be used. In any case, it presents an easy and unusual side salad.

12 oz (350 g) radishes, thinly sliced
1 small onion, grated
3 tablespoons olive oil
salt and pepper to taste

1. Trim the radishes and slice them thinly, or grate them.
2. Mix in the remaining ingredients. Blend well.

Serves 4

Radish and Orange Salad

Try this for a Moroccan salad with an exotic tang.

4 oranges
large bunch of radishes, sliced
juice of half a lemon
3 tablespoons olive oil
3 garlic cloves, crushed
salt
6-12 black olives
1 teaspoon paprika
pinch of cayenne pepper
½-1 teaspoon cumin (optional)

1. Peel the oranges and cut them into slices, then pieces. Place in a bowl together with the sliced radishes.
2. Combine the lemon juice, olive oil, garlic, and salt and add to the oranges and radishes. Mix in the olives and toss it all together.
3. Sprinkle with paprika, cayenne pepper—and cumin, if you want to.

Serves 6

Cauliflower and Radish Salad

Your guests will enjoy this crunchy and uncommon salad with its surprisingly superb blend of ingredients.

1 small cauliflower
8-10 radishes, sliced
small red Spanish onion (or half a medium onion), chopped
3 tablespoons chili ketchup
4 tablespoons mayonnaise
1 teaspoon chopped fresh dill or ½ teaspoon dried dill
parsley (optional)

1. Break the cauliflower into florets and cut into smaller pieces (about 1 inch or 2.5 cm).
2. Place the cauliflower in a bowl with the radishes and onion.
3. Mix together the chili ketchup, mayonnaise and dill and add to the vegetables. Toss together until well mixed. Garnish with chopped parsley if you want to.

6 servings

Marinated Radish Salad

Serve in a clear glass bowl to display the looks of this colorful and tangy salad.

about 1 lb (450 g) radishes
4 fl oz (100 ml or ½ cup) white wine vinegar
2 teaspoons salt
olive oil to taste
freshly ground black pepper
2 tablespoons capers
1 green chili pepper, cut into strips

1. Wash and slice the radishes. Marinate them in vinegar and salt for about three hours. Drain.
2. Place the radishes in a salad bowl and mix with olive oil and freshly ground pepper to taste.
3. Sprinkle capers and chili pepper over the top to garnish.

Serves 4

Middle Eastern Salad

Here is an especially attractive—and refreshing—salad to augment a meal.

1 long or 2 short cucumbers
4 medium tomatoes
10-12 radishes, sliced
2 green peppers, diced
1 bunch spring onions, chopped
bunch of parsley, chopped
juice of 1 small lemon
¼ teaspoon pepper
4 fl oz (100 ml or ½ cup) oil

1. Cut cucumbers and tomatoes into ½-inch (1.5 cm) chunks.
2. Prepare all the vegetables and place them in a salad bowl.
3. Mix together the lemon juice and pepper and, with a whisk, gradually beat in the oil.
4. Toss the dressing with the vegetables and serve.

Serves 6

Chinese Radish Salad

Here is a salad that goes particularly well with barbecued dishes.

30 radishes, sliced
1½ green peppers, slivered
3 tablespoons soy sauce
3 tablespoons rice or wine vinegar
1 tablespoon sugar (or less)

1. Combine all ingredients.
2. Chill thoroughly and serve.

Serves 4-5

Radish Salad with Minted Peas

An agreeable spring salad with attractive color contrast. Do not use too much mint as the flavor should be subtle, not dominating. You may also use 1 tablespoon of chopped fresh dill in place of the mint.

**1 cup water
1 lb (450 g) shelled peas
1 large bunch radishes, thinly sliced
1 spring onion or scallion, thinly sliced
stalk celery, chopped
1 teaspoon fresh mint, finely chopped
1 tablespoon mayonnaise
2 tablespoons sour cream or crème fraîche
freshly ground black pepper to taste**

1. Add peas to a saucepan of boiling salted water and cook until they are just tender, about 4 minutes for fresh peas. Run cold water over them right away to stop them cooking. Drain well.
2. Mix peas with radishes, spring onion, celery, and mint. (Do not add salt, which will cause radishes to give off liquid.) Place in refrigerator and chill for at least one hour.
3. Before serving, mix in the mayonnaise, sour cream or crème fraîche, and pepper.
4. Serve on a bed of lettuce and garnish with wedges of tomato if you want to.

Serves 4-6

Boiled Radishes

This is a simple recipe for radishes, which lose their pungent flavor and take on a milder taste when cooked.

1. Cut off the roots and tops, leaving just a little bit of the top stalk, and wash well in cold water.
2. Boil or steam large whole radishes for about 9-12 minutes.
3. Serve with butter, salt and pepper, or with a cream sauce, or a seasoned parsley sauce.

Sautéed Radishes

The cooked radishes in this dish have a milder taste than raw radishes, and the recipe yields an attractive color combination.

2 large bunches radishes, sliced
3 tablespoons butter
small bunch spring onions, cut into ¼-inch (.5 cm) slices
1 medium courgette (zucchini), cut into sticks about 2 inches (5 cm) long
summer squash (an equal amount to courgette), cut into sticks about 2 inches (5 cm) long
salt and pepper to taste
chopped fresh basil, dill, or parsley to garnish

1. In a large frying pan, melt the butter over medium heat. Add unpeeled, sliced radishes and spring onions and sauté for 1 minute.
2. Add courgettes and squash, salt and pepper, and continue to cook for another 3 to 4 minutes, until radishes are pink and vegetables are tender.
3. Sprinkle with a fresh herb and serve.

Serves 4-6

Braised Radishes

Braising them in butter is an excellent cooking method for radishes.

2 tablespoons butter
1 tablespoon vegetable oil
1 lb (450 g) radishes, trimmed
salt and pepper
2 fl oz (50 ml or ¼ cup) chicken stock or white wine
1 tablespoon vinegar, preferably raspberry vinegar
1 teaspoon sugar
chopped fresh parsley to garnish

1. Place the butter and oil in a large frying pan on medium heat. When butter melts, add radishes.
2. Cook for a few minutes, stirring to coat radishes with butter. Add salt and pepper to taste.
3. Stir in other ingredients, except parsley, mix, and cover the pan. Cook on low heat for about 5 minutes or until radishes are just about tender.
4. Remove cover and continue to cook on medium heat for a few minutes, stirring until the radishes are glazed and the liquid thickens. Adjust seasonings.
5. Spoon into a serving dish and sprinkle with chopped parsley to garnish.

Serves 4

Radishes in Mustard Sauce

This wintry dish is especially great with roasts.

about 3 lbs (1.4 kg) radishes
1 tablespoon olive oil
salt and freshly ground black pepper
8 fl oz (225 ml or 1 cup) stock (chicken, beef, or vegetable)
2 teaspoons cornstarch
3 tablespoons Dijon mustard
chopped fresh parsley for garnish

1. Trim radishes and cut in half if they are large.
2. Place oil in a large frying pan on medium heat. Add the radishes. Sprinkle in salt and pepper. Cook for a few minutes, stirring occasionally.
3. Add stock and cover the pan. Simmer until radishes are tender, about 5 minutes.
4. Take the radishes out of the pan with a slotted spoon, and place them in a serving dish. Keep them warm.
5. Mix together the cornstarch and mustard and stir the mixture into liquid in the pan. Cook over low heat to thicken it a bit, then pour the sauce over the radishes. Garnish with parsley and serve.

Serves 6

Salsify

SALSIFY

Definitely one of the less common vegetables, salsify, a long tapering root, is closely related to scorzonera and members of the same family as dandelion and lettuce. It usually has a white or pale brownish skin but can also have a black or grayish skin in which case it is called scorzonera or black salsify. Both have pale creamy flesh and are similar in flavor, which is somewhat like artichokes and asparagus. Salsify is also sometimes referred to as the oyster plant because its taste has been compared to oysters.

Native to the Mediterranean, salsify now grows in Europe and North America. Historically, it has been used in medicines for the treatment of heartburn, loss of appetite and a variety of liver diseases.

Preparation is difficult. To prepare, either scrub the root under cold running water and peel after cooking, or peel with a sharp knife and place the trimmed pieces into acidulated water (water with lemon juice added), as the flesh discolors quickly. This root vegetable can be creamed or fried in butter or used in soups. It can be cooked like carrots, parsnips, or potatoes.

RECIPES for SALSIFY

SIDE DISHES

Boiled Salsify

You can embellish a basic dish of salsify by simply adding butter and parsley or lemon juice. Or use a white or Bernaise sauce.

1 lb (450 g) salsify
butter
chopped parsley
lemon juice (optional)

1. Prepare by scrubbing and cutting off tops and root ends. Peel or scrape off skin and cut into lengths 1-2 inches (2.5-5 cm). Place pieces immediately in acidulated water (water with lemon juice added) to keep them from discoloring.
2. Place in boiling water, then lower heat and cook for about 40 minutes until tender.
3. Drain. Toss in butter and parsley. Add lemon juice if you want to and serve.

Serves 4

Sautéed Salsify

This is an alternative and easy method of cooking salsify to make a pleasant accompaniment.

1 lb (450 g) salsify
butter
lemon juice
chopped parsley

1. Prepare salsify. Peel skin off and cut into short lengths, immediately putting the pieces into acidulated water.
2. Boil water in a saucepan, then lower the heat and simmer vegetables for 25-30 minutes until tender. Drain.
3. Sauté the salsify in butter in a frying pan.
4. Add lemon juice. Garnish with chopped parsley and serve.

Serves 4

Salsify Gratin

Spinach is used in this recipe to augment the quantity as well as the color of this little-known root vegetable. But if you opt to patiently peel a lot of salsify, use less spinach—or leave it out.

1 lb (450 g) salsify, cut into 2-inch (5 cm) lengths
juice of 1 lemon
1 lb (450 g) spinach
5 fl oz (150 ml) chicken or vegetable stock
10 fl oz (300 ml) single or light cream
salt and freshly ground black pepper

1. Trim off the tops and bottoms and peel off the skin of the salsify. Cut and plunge each piece immediately in acidulated water to prevent discoloration.
2. Place the salsify with the lemon juice in a saucepan of boiling water, then simmer for about 15 minutes or until it is just tender. Drain.
3. Cook the spinach in a large saucepan for 2-3 minutes.
4. Pour the stock and cream into a small saucepan and add the seasonings. Gently heat through while stirring.
5. In a buttered ovenproof baking dish, arrange the salsify and spinach in layers. Pour the stock and cream mixture over it.
6. Bake in preheated oven at 325°F (160°C) for about 1 hour until top is golden brown.

Serves 6

Swedes or Rutabagas

SWEDES or RUTABAGAS

The swede (also known as Swedish turnip) is a root vegetable that is known in the United States as rutabaga or yellow turnip. The name goes back to the late eighteenth century when Sweden began exporting the vegetable to Britain.

Swedes are winter vegetables that are similar to turnips and treated like them, but they are larger and have tougher skins than turnips and require a sharp paring knife to peel the thick skin. Also, they have a milder flavor and yellow-orange flesh (and are therefore sometimes referred to as yellow turnips). Like all root vegetables, they store well and can be used in any turnip recipe.

Although swedes, like turnips, have been around for centuries, they have not been considered gourmet food. On the contrary, they have had a reputation as a staple for poorer families. But in recent times, swedes and turnips have been gaining in esteem as new ways of cooking them are presented.

Small swedes with unblemished and smooth skins are best. Large ones may be fibrous. They must not be overcooked or they will fall apart.

With their sweet taste, and with their ability to absorb other flavors well, swedes or rutabagas are excellent partners to other vegetables or in casseroles and stews. They are even good eaten raw, as in a salad. Take advantage of their sweetish flavor to make a cheerful winter salad by mixing coarsely-grated Swedes together with mayonnaise and chopped dates in proportions to suit yourself.

And they are nutritious—a good source of calcium and potassium.

RECIPES for SWEDES OR RUTABAGAS

Buttered Swedes

These boiled swedes may also be mashed with butter, nutmeg and ginger.

2 lbs (1 kg) swedes
2 oz (50 g) butter
salt and pepper

1. Prepare swedes by trimming stalk and root ends. Peel to remove the skin and cut into small cubes.
2. Boil in salted water for 30 minutes or until tender when pierced with a skewer. Drain thoroughly.
3. Toss with melted butter and seasonings.

Serves 6

Bashed Neaps

*A traditional Scottish dish for swedes or rutabagas—or turnips—
simply mashes them with carrots or potatoes. The dish is served
with haggis at traditional Burns Night suppers in Scotland,
where they are referred to as bashed neaps.*

swedes, turnips, carrots, potatoes
butter
black pepper

Simply cook the vegetables and mash them together with lots of
butter and freshly ground black pepper.

Swede and Carrot Purée

The mixture of these two vegetables works extremely well to produce a marvelous dish. (But it can also be made without the carrots.)

1 lb (450 g) swedes
1 lb (450 g) carrots
1 medium onion, peeled and sliced
4 garlic cloves
1 oz (25 g) butter
nutmeg
pinch of cinnamon or allspice

1. Peel the swede and cut into cubes. Peel and slice the carrots. Place vegetables in saucepan of boiling water and cook for about 20 minutes, or until tender.
2. Place onion and garlic cloves in a food processor or blender. Add the vegetables and process until it has the consistency of mashed potatoes. Blend in the butter.
3. Mix in some nutmeg to taste and a pinch of cinnamon or allspice.
4. Transfer to a serving dish or casserole, heat thoroughly, and serve.

Serves 6

Custardy Swede Casserole

The appealing flavor of this custard-like casserole makes it a great choice to serve for a holiday dinner. It may well become an all-time favorite.

1 swede (about 1 lb or 500 g)
2 eggs, well beaten
8 fl oz (225 ml or 1 cup) light cream, scalded
2 tablespoons butter
2 tablespoons brown sugar
pinch or two of nutmeg
salt to taste

1. Peel the swede and cut it into small cubes. Boil in salted water for about 30 minutes. Drain well and purée in a blender or food processor.
2. Beat the eggs, then beat in the puréed swede. Add the rest of the ingredients and mix well.
3. Turn the mixture into a buttered casserole, and place the casserole in a shallow pan. Fill the pan with hot water to a depth of 1 inch (2.5 cm).
4. Place in oven preheated to 350°F (180°C) and bake for about 1 hour or until it is set.
5. Allow to sit for 10 minutes before serving.

Serves 6

219

Golden Rutabaga with Shallots

Makes an exquisite departure from standard fare.

1½ lbs (700 g) rutabaga, peeled and cubed
1 tablespoon butter
12 shallots, peeled and halved
8 fl oz (225 ml or 1 cup) chicken broth
4 fl oz (100 ml or ½ cup) dry sherry or Madeira
2 tablespoons honey
¼ teaspoon salt
¼ teaspoon fresh thyme
¼ teaspoon freshly ground fresh pepper

1. Use a sharp paring knife to peel the thick and tough skin. Cut rutabaga into 1-inch (2.5 cm) cubes. Place the cubes in a large saucepan. Cover with water and bring to a boil. Lower heat and simmer 25 minutes, until tender. Drain.
2. While rutabaga is cooking, melt butter in a large pan over medium heat. Add shallots and sauté for 2 minutes. Add chicken broth, sherry, honey, and salt. Bring to a boil, then reduce heat and simmer about 20 minutes or until mixture is reduced by half.
3. Add thyme and pepper and rutabaga cubes. Mix together gently and serve.

Serves 6

Julienne of Root Vegetables

Yellow swede, white turnip, and orange carrots make a colorful mixture. But you could use just two of these—or add another vegetable.

10 oz (300 g) swede, peeled
10 oz (300 g) turnips, peeled
10 oz (300 g) carrots, scraped
1 oz (25 g) butter
salt and freshly ground black pepper
parsley to garnish

1. Cut the vegetables into julienne strips. Place them in a saucepan covered with cold water and bring to a boil.
2. Cook gently, half covering the pan, for about 10 minutes or until the vegetables are just tender.
3. Drain. Add butter to the vegetables and season with salt and freshly ground pepper. Turn into a serving dish and sprinkle with chopped parsley.

Serves 4-6

Piquant Swedes

You can, of course, use turnips instead—or a combination.

1 lb (450 g) swedes
2 oz (50 g) butter
1 small onion, finely chopped
2 tablespoons sugar
2 tablespoons wine vinegar
salt and pepper
2 teaspoons grated horseradish
½ teaspoon grated orange rind

1. Prepare the swedes and cut them into small cubes. Boil until tender but crisp. Drain.
2. Melt butter in a large frying pan. Add onion and fry gently.
3. Stir in remaining ingredients and season to taste.
4. Cook and stir in the vegetable cubes.

Serves 6

Baked Swedes

Perfect accompaniment to a Sunday roast.

1 lb (450 g) swedes
1 oz (25 g) butter
1 tablespoon vegetable oil

1. Prepare swedes and cut them into longish chunks.
2. Heat the butter and oil in the oven in a roasting pan. While it is heating, blanch the swedes in boiling water for 3 minutes. Drain.
3. Remove pan when fat is hot and sizzling and place it on direct heat. Add swedes. As soon as each touches the fat, turn over with tongs to coat the whole surface.
4. Replace the pan in oven preheated at 400°F (200°C) and bake for about 40 minutes. Turn them over about halfway through, until they are golden brown.

Serves 4

Swedes with Honey

It gets easier and easier to cook and love this root vegetable.

1 lb (450 g) swedes
2 tablespoons clear honey

1. Prepare the swedes and cut into cubes. Boil for about 30 minutes or until tender but still crisp.
2. Drain and replace them in the saucepan over low heat to evaporate any excess water.
3. Add clear runny honey—as much as you like. Heat quickly. Stir and serve.

Serves 6

Turnips

TURNIPS

Turnips were traditionally poor people's food because they are easy to grow and can be stored for a long time. But they are delicious and tender and enjoyable. Kept in the vegetable bin, lightly wrapped in plastic, they will keep for weeks. Turnips should be firm and undamaged. They should also be small, as larger ones (more than two inches or 5 cm in diameter) may be woody.

Early and maincrop are the two types of this root vegetable. Early turnips have tender flesh and may be eaten raw (unexpectedly delicious in salads) or cooked. The small purple-tinged turnips that arrive in early June are a real treat when properly cooked. They cook quickly and are ideal to sauté. Maincrop turnips, the larger winter variety, are a bit coarser and generally cut into chunks. Stews, casseroles, and soups are the usual way to go for these tasty, yet inexpensive vegetables.

To prepare, wash, trim ends, and peel. Small ones can be left whole; large turnips should be quartered. If boiling, allow 25-30 minutes. They are great roasted with duck. A traditional Scottish method (See Bashed Neeps, page 217) is to simply whip them with lots of butter and black pepper—delicious! In Wales they combine potatoes and turnips and call it Punchnep.

RECIPES for TURNIPS

Turnip Soup

An amazingly good soup to make when the first white turnips of the season appear in May.

4-5 white turnips, peeled and diced
32 fl oz (950 ml) beef broth
8 fl oz (225 ml or 1 cup) heavy cream
salt and pepper to taste
2 egg yolks, beaten
1 tablespoon butter

1. Prepare turnips (about 2 cups) and cook them in the beef broth until tender. Remove the turnips with a slotted spoon and reserve the broth.
2. Purée the turnips in a food processor or blender.
3. Add the puréed turnips to the reserved broth and bring to a boil, then remove from heat. Add the cream and the salt and freshly ground black pepper.
4. Reheat being careful not to boil. Remove from heat.
5. Stir in the beaten egg yolks and butter. Serve hot.

Serves 6

French Turnip Soup

Another turnip soup recipe for those young and tasty white turnips, which the French often combine with other root vegetables for a creamy soup.

¾ lb (350 g) turnips, peeled and diced
½ lb (225 g) potatoes, peeled and diced
1 leek, trimmed and chopped
1 onion, chopped
2 oz (50 g) butter
1 oz (25 g) flour
40 fl oz (1.2 litres) vegetable stock
salt and freshly ground black pepper
2 egg yolks
3 tablespoons heavy or double cream

1. Dice the turnips and potatoes. Remove roots and coarse outer leaves from the leek, cut it in half and rinse thoroughly to remove dirt, and chop coarsely. Chop the onion.
2. In a large pan melt the butter and add the vegetables. Cook over low heat, covered, for about 10 minutes, until vegetables are tender but not browned. Add the flour and cook and stir a few minutes longer. Add the stock gradually, blending it all together. Season with salt and pepper.
3. Simmer over low heat until vegetables are tender, about 30 minutes. Allow to cool a little.
4. Purée in a blender or food processor. Reheat over low heat.
5. In a small bowl, beat egg yolks with the cream, then mix in a little of the hot soup. Pour it all back into the soup and continue to stir for a few minutes over low heat, but be careful not to boil.
6. Serve hot, with a bowl of croutons to be passed around.

Serves 6-8

Punchnep

A delicious combination of whipped turnips and potatoes that makes a Welsh treat.

1 lb (450 g) turnips, peeled and cut into chunks
1 lb (450 g) potatoes, peeled and cut into chunks
1 oz (25 g) butter
salt and pepper
3 fl oz (75 ml) light cream

1. In a large saucepan, cook the turnips on their own for 5 minutes (as they take longer to cook than potatoes). Add potatoes and cook both vegetables together for 25 minutes until they are tender.
2. Drain the vegetables and turn them into a bowl. Add the butter and seasonings. Mash or beat them in an electric mixer. When they are well whipped, turn the mixture into a serving dish or casserole. You may stop at this point and continue later with the last step when you are ready for final preparations.
3. Heat vegetable mixture. Warm the cream gently in a saucepan.
4. Form several holes in the vegetable mixture by moving a spoon handle or other instrument around in a circle. Pour the hot cream into the holes and serve immediately.

Serves 6

Fried Sliced Turnips

A different way to use your turnips.

6 white turnips, peeled and thinly sliced
1 egg
1 teaspoon water
3 tablespoons olive oil
3 tablespoons flour
salt

1. Partially cook turnip slices in boiling salted water. Drain and dry them on paper towels.
2. Beat egg and water together.
3. Heat the oil in a heavy frying pan. Dip turnip slices first in flour, then in egg. Fry them in hot oil until they are crispy brown.
4. Drain on paper towels, season to taste with salt, and serve hot.

Serves 6

Grated Turnips

A dish that is liked even by people who normally don't like turnips.

1 lb (450 g) fresh turnips, grated
2 tablespoons oil
1 medium-large onion, chopped
1 large clove garlic, chopped
salt and black pepper, to taste

1. Peel turnips and grate them on a medium grater or in a food processor.
2. Place oil in a frying pan, and sauté the onions over medium heat until they are tender, about 10 minutes.
3. Add garlic and continue to sauté for another few minutes.
4. Add the grated turnips and season with salt and pepper. Cover and cook over low heat, stirring from time to time, for about 15-20 minutes.

Serves 4

Turnips with Mustard Sauce

Another tangy dish that may convert many people who avoid turnips to enthusiastic consumers of this vegetable.

2 lbs (1 kg) turnips or swedes or a combination
2 oz (50 g) butter
1-2 teaspoons strong French mustard
salt and pepper to taste
2 tablespoons lemon juice
chopped parsley to garnish

1. Slice turnips and cook them in boiling water for about 25-30 minutes or until tender. Remove them with a slotted spoon to a serving bowl and keep warm. Reserve the water.
2. Melt butter, and add mustard and a very small amount of the hot turnip water. Whisk together until well blended. Season with salt and pepper. Combine this mixture with the turnip slices.
3. Add a sprinkling of lemon juice and chopped parsley over the top and serve.

Serves 6-8

Turnips with Sour Cream

Another variation!

6 turnips
1 tablespoon caraway seeds
2 fl oz (50 ml or ¼ cup) sour cream
½ teaspoon dried basil
paprika
lemon juice

1. Put the turnips in boiling water with the caraway seeds and cook for 10 minutes. Drain and cool.
2. Peel the turnips and slice them. Gently mix in the sour cream and basil and put into a buttered casserole. Cover and bake in a preheated oven at 350°F (180°C) for about 25 minutes, until they are tender.
3. Shake some paprika over the top and a bit of lemon juice and serve.

Serves 6

Turnip and Swede Medley

There is something comforting and warming about this dish of root vegetables, which are best appreciated in winter.

1 lb (450 g) turnips
1 lb (450 g) swedes
salt and pepper to taste
bundle of watercress, chopped
1-2 tablespoons heavy or double cream

1. Peel and dice vegetables and boil them until tender.
2. Turn them into a casserole. Season with salt and pepper. Mix in the watercress and cream.

Serves 6

Mashed Turnip Casserole

Another casserole for your turnip repertory.

1½ lbs (700 g or 3 cups) mashed turnips
3 tablespoons butter
3 teaspoons sugar
1 teaspoon salt
½ teaspoon freshly ground black pepper
8 oz (225 g) soft bread crumbs
2 eggs, beaten
1 tablespoon butter, melted

1. Mix together the turnips, butter, sugar, salt, pepper, half the bread crumbs and the eggs. Spoon the mixture into a buttered casserole.
2. Mix remaining crumbs with the melted butter and spread this mixture over the top.
3. Bake in preheated oven at 350°F (180°C) for about 30-35 minutes, until top is browned.

Serves 4-6

Turnips and Leeks Boulangère

Like Potatoes Boulangère, the name of this dish derives from the French bread ovens that villagers used for cooking their pots of turnips and other vegetables.

2 lbs (1 kg) turnips, thinly sliced
1 large leek, chopped
salt and pepper to taste
5 fl oz (150 ml) stock
5 fl oz (150 ml) milk
1 oz (25 g) butter

1. Place a layer of turnips in a well-buttered baking dish. Sprinkle some of the chopped leeks over it and salt and pepper. Continue alternating layers, ending with turnips on top.
2. Pour in stock and milk. Top with bits of butter.
3. Bake in preheated oven at 350°F (180°C) for about 45 minutes or until turnips are tender and top layer is golden.

Serves 4-6

Roasted Turnips and Root Vegetables

This low cholesterol, highly flavorful, and heart-healthy dish can use a combination of almost any vegetable, but don't omit carrots, onions, or garlic.

2 lbs (1 kg) mixed root vegetables (turnips, carrots, potatoes, sweet potatoes, parsnips, whole shallots, onions)
4 tablespoons olive oil
several sprigs fresh thyme or 1 tablespoon fresh rosemary leaves
salt and pepper
1 head garlic, broken into cloves
chopped parsley for garnish

1. Cut vegetables into 2-inch (5 cm) chunks.
2. Measure oil into a roasting pan and place on top of stove on low heat. Add all vegetables except garlic. Add herbs and sprinkle with salt and pepper. Cook for a few minutes, stirring to coat all the vegetables with oil. Place the pan in an oven preheated to 425°F (210 °C).
3. Roast for 30 minutes, stirring gently from time to time, until vegetables start to brown.
4. Stir the garlic cloves into the vegetables. Continue roasting and stirring occasionally until vegetables are tender and brown, about 30 minutes. (If they do not brown, place under broiler for a minute or two.)
5. Turn into a serving bowl and garnish with parsley.

Serves 4-6

Gourmet Turnip Entrée

A perfect blend of spices makes this a pleasurable repast that may be eaten on its own or over cooked rice.

**1 tablespoon vegetable oil
3 cloves garlic, chopped
1 medium-large onion, coarsely chopped
3-4 turnips, peeled and cut into ½ inch (1.2 cm) cubes
2 medium carrots, cut into ½ inch (1.2 cm) slices
10-12 medium-size mushrooms, cut into quarters
½ teaspoon dried thyme
¼ teaspoon dried tarragon
1 bay leaf
salt and pepper to taste
4 fl oz (100 ml or ½ cup) water or stock
fresh chopped parsley**

1. Place oil in a large saucepan over moderate heat. Add all ingredients except the water and parsley and cook, stirring frequently, for 5 minutes.
2. Add water or stock and parsley, then reduce heat to low and continue to cook, covered, until vegetables are tender, about 20 minutes.
3. Discard bay leaf. Sprinkle fresh chopped parsley over the top if you want to and serve.

Serves 6

Root Vegetable Pie

*If you are gathering a lot of root vegetable produce from your
own garden plot, this dish will enable you to enjoy your good
fortune. It makes a pleasant change and is a special treat for
vegetarians.*

**2 lbs (1 kg) root vegetables—a mixture of turnips, swedes,
carrots, potatoes, parsnips, onions, Jerusalem artichokes
salt and freshly ground pepper to taste
a handful of chopped parsley
2 oz (50 g) butter
2 oz (50 g) flour
8 oz (225 g) grated cheese
milk
shortcrust pastry**

1. Peel vegetables and cut into cubes. Boil for 5 minutes in salted
   water. Drain, reserving the water.
2. Arrange the vegetables in a large pie dish. Season with salt
   and pepper and mix in the parsley.
3. Blend together the butter, flour and grated cheese with a little
   milk and enough vegetable water to make a sauce that is as
   thick as cream. Pour the sauce over the vegetables.
4. Cover with shortcrust pastry and bake in a hot oven at 425°F
   (210°C) for 35 minutes. Lower heat to 300°F (150°C) and
   bake for an additional hour.

Serves 6

NOTES

TABLE OF WEIGHTS AND MEASURES

Teaspoon and Tablespoon measurements are level.

LIQUID EQUIVALENTS
1 litre = 1000 ml = 1¾ Imperial pints = 2 US pints = 4 cups

600 ml = 1 Imperial pint = 1¼ US pints = 2½ cups

½ litre = 500 ml = ¾ Imperial pint = 1 US pint = 2 cups

300 ml = ½ Imperial pint = 1¼ cups

¼ litre = 250 ml = 8 fl oz = ½ US pint = 1 cup

150 ml = 5 fl oz = 2/3 cup

100-125 ml = 3 ½-4 fl oz = 1/3-½ cup

WEIGHTS
28 g = 1 oz

110 g = 4 oz or ½ cup

225 g = 8 oz or 1 cup

450 g = 16 oz or 1 lb

1 kg = 2 lbs